The Practical Guitar Method

By: Donovan Raitt

Copyright 2008-2016 Donovan Raitt Music. All Rights Reserved.
Unauthorized Duplication is a violation of applicable copyright laws and is
prohibited.

Table of Contents

The Parts of the Guitar

Electric Guitar

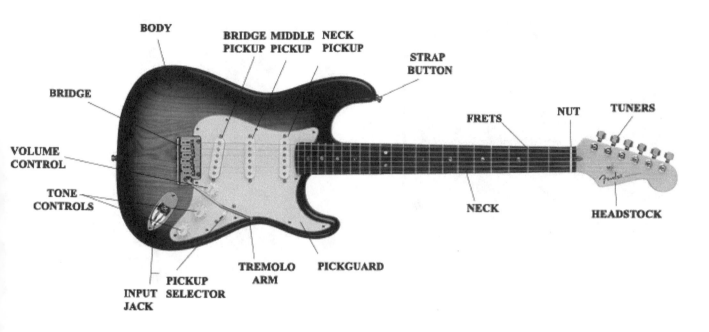

Acoustic Guitar

Holding the Guitar

The guitar can be played sitting down or standing up using a strap. When sitting down, the guitar should rest between your thigh and underarm with your elbow wrapped around the horn of the guitar as seen in the picture below. When using a guitar strap, place both your head and picking hand through the strap, and adjust the strap so the guitar is at a comfortable height.

Sitting Position   **Standing Position**

Holding the Pick

The pick should be held between the thumb and the index finger of your right hand. Put your hand in a "thumbs up" position and rest the pick as shown on your index finger. The pointed end should be facing away from your fist. Place the thumb so your fingertip is in the middle of the pick and only the end of the pick sticks out. Make sure your hand is relaxed, as too much tension in your hand can slow down your picking.

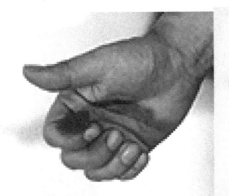

Rest the pick on top of your index finger. Press down with your thumb. Make sure your hand is relaxed.

Numbering the Frets and Left Hand Position

The **Frets,** or pieces of metal running across the guitar neck separate notes on the guitar from each other. When we press down on the guitar, we press on the wood between the two frets to play each note. Each fret is numbered from the 1st fret closest to the headstock, and run up to between 20 and 24 frets depending on the design of your instrument.

Numbering the Strings

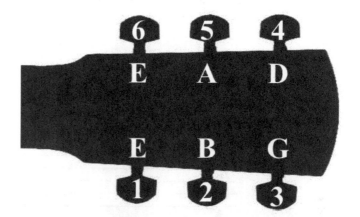

The strings on the guitar are numbered from the thickest and lowest pitch string (6th), which is closest to you looking down at the guitar, to the thinnest and highest pitch string (1st), which is furthest away.

Tuning the Guitar

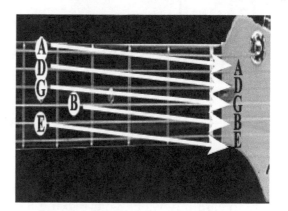

In order to tune the guitar, the easiest method would be to use an electronic tuner. The guitar is tuned from the thickest string to the thinnest string. You can tune each string by pressing the 5th fret of the lowest string and checking to see if it matches the open 5th string. This works for all of the strings except for the 2nd string, which is tuned using the 4th fret of the 3rd string.

Left Hand Fingering

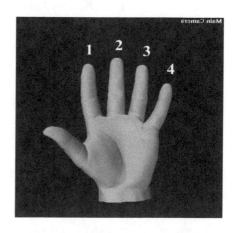

Because we do not use the thumb to play the guitar, your index finger is your 1st finger, your middle finger is your 2nd finger, your ring finger is your 3rd finger and your pinky is your 4th finger.

Reading Tablature

Tablature is a system of shorthand music notation for the guitar that uses numbers to indicate where notes are found on the guitar. Tablature notation was first seen in the lute music of the 16th and 17th centuries, and is still commonly used today. A tablature staff has six lines, each one representing a string on the guitar.

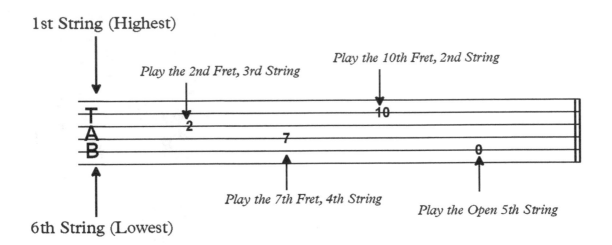

Alternate Picking

The following exercises are designed to make alternate picking (the combination of upward and downward pick strokes) easier in order to play melodies and solos quickly and efficiently. Make sure to carefully watch your picking hand to make sure you are alternating the pick for each note. Most of the exercises in this book will be played using alternate picking, so study it well!

Pick Symbols and Picking Directions

This symbol is a picking direction indicator. When you see this symbol,   pick the string toward the ground. This is called a *Downstroke.*

If you see this symbol   V   pick in the opposite direction. This is called an *Upstroke.*

Part 1: Open String Alternate Picking

These exercises are to help you concentrate on your picking hand by playing the open strings. Use a metronome at a slow tempo so you have control over your hand at all times. Try not to look at your hand as you play these exercises, as you will not be able to look at both of your hands and the music at the same time.

Exercise 1

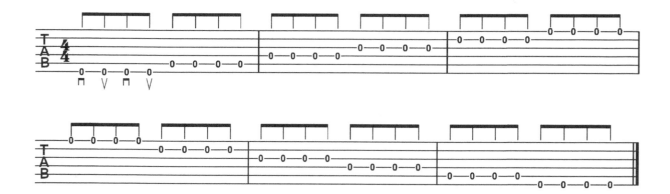

Exercise 2

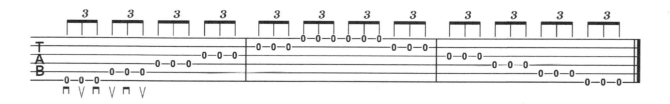

Part 2: Skipping Strings

Now we are going to concentrate on skipping strings with our picking hand. This can be very tricky to do in the middle of the song, but with these exercises you should have no problem training your hand to move the distance required to skip a string.

Exercise 1

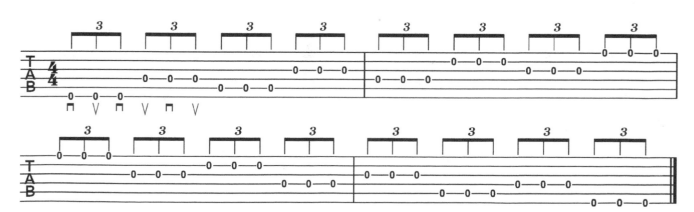

Exercise 2

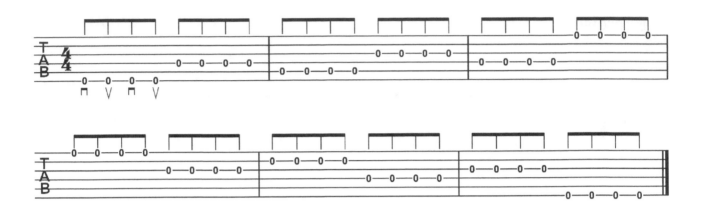

Part 3: Adding the Left Hand

Now that we are comfortable with our picking hand on its own, it is time to add your fretting hand into the equation. It will take time to learn to synchronize your two hands together, but with patience and practice it will get easier.

Exercise 1

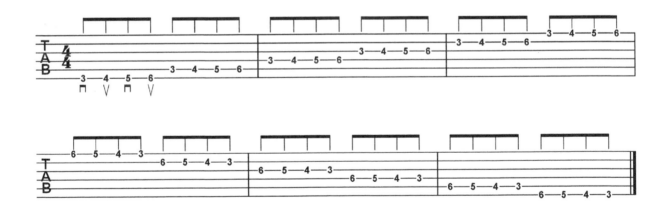

Exercise 2

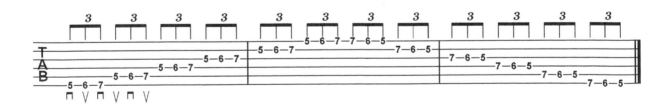

CHAPTER 1 - READING MUSIC

Before we can start to learn how to play the guitar, we must first learn how to read and understand the musical examples found in the following exercises and lessons. Music notation may seem tricky at first, but with patience and perseverance you will discover that it is much easier than you originally thought.

Standard Notation

Other than tablature, the most common system of guitar notation is called *Standard Notation*. This form of notation is used among all instruments, including brass, woodwinds, and stringed instruments. *Standard Notation* uses a group of five lines called a *Staff* to notate the movement of pitch (unlike tablature which only shows the fretboard location) of the music.

Treble Clef

The *Treble Clef* tells us what each line on the staff represents. Notice the *Treble Clef* looks like the letter G. This is because the 2nd line where the clef curls around represents the note G. From this point, we can tell what each note is in reference to the 2nd line.

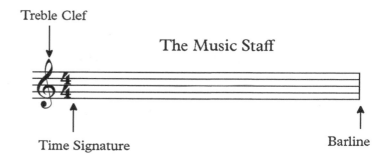

Notes

The higher up the note is placed on the staff, the higher the sounding pitch of the note, and the lower the placement on the staff, the lower the sounding pitch of that note. This system allows us to visualize the change in pitch of each note. Each note rests on the staff either on a line or on a space between two lines.

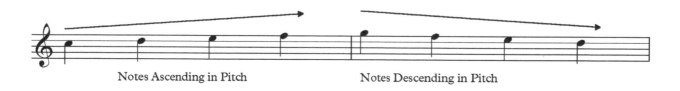

Notes Ascending in Pitch   Notes Descending in Pitch

Because of the *Treble Clef,* we are able to determine which note each line or space represents. The line notes are easily remembered by the phrase "**E**very **G**ood **B**oy **D**oes **F**ine," while the space notes spell the word **"FACE."**

Rhythm

Even if we know the correct notes of a song, they need to be played in the correct rhythm. **Rhythm is defined as the amount of time that each note is heard.** In order to notate rhythm, we need to indicate the length of each note in the music.

Whole Note	Half Note	Quarter Note	Eigth Note
4 Beats	2 Beats	1 Beat	1/2 Beat

Time Signature

A *Time Signature* is used to determine the pulse of the music.

The upper number on the time signature tells us **how many beats are in a measure.** The lower number indicates **which type of note rhythm is counted as 1 beat**

In the first measure below, the number "4" on the top would indicate that there are 4 beats of time in that measure. In the second measure, the "3" on the top would indicate three beats of time.

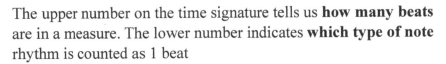

In the measures below, the number "4" on the top would indicate that there are 4 beats of time in each measure. Notice the bottom number has changed in each measure, and therefore the count is represented by different note values. the "4" on the bottom number indicates quarter notes get the beat, while the "2" indicates half notes, and the "8" indicates half notes.

Open String Notes

These Each open string on the guitar is represented by a note on the treble staff. By learning to recognize these notes and connect them to the open strings, we will be able to learn how to connect open position notes on the guitar to their location on the treble staff.

Exercise 1

Exercise 2

Exercise 3

Exercise 4

Exercise 5

Rhythmic Exercises

The following exercises are designed to help you with counting and playing rhythms. The note that is used in these exercises is the note E, which is played on the open 1st string (thinnest string of the guitar)

Exercise 1

Exercise 2

Exercise 3

Exercise 4

Exercise 5

Rests

A *Rest* is a symbol that tells the musician to stop playing for a short period of time. Just as there are different durations of notes, there are different durations of rests. These types are *Whole Rests, Half Rests, Quarter Rests,* and *Eighth Rests.* Just as a *Whole Note* lasts for 4 beats of time, a *Whole Rest* will last for 4 beats as well. *Half Rests* will last for two beats, and so on.

Practice the following exercises to get comfortable playing music using rests. Remember that all of the strings need to be stopped so there is no sound for the entire duration of the rest.

Exercise 1

Exercise 2

Exercise 3

Tied Rhythms

A *Tie* connects two notes so that when the first note is played, it is held for the duration of the original note as well as the tied note.

Excerpt from "Invention No. 1" by: J.S Bach

Dotted Rhythms

We can use dotted rhythms to extend the value of a note. A Dot (.) added to a note ADDS HALF THE VALUE of the previous note. For example, a half note with a dot next to it would be held for 3 beats. Observe the following examples of each of these dotted notes

A dotted quarter note is the same value
as a quarter note tied to an eigth note

A dotted half note is the same value
as a half note tied to an quarter note

Excerpt from "Orchestral Suite #2" by: J.S Bach

Excerpt from "Orchestral Suite #3" by: J.S Bach

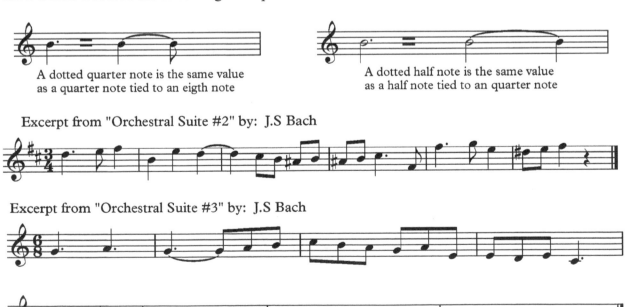

Other Musical Symbols

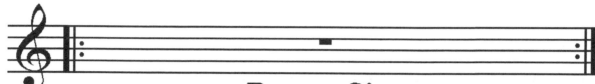

Repeat Sign
*Markers placed at the beginning and end
of a repeated section of music.*

Ending Markers
*Designates a change in the ending of a repeated section.
The first ending is skipped on the repeat and the second ending is played instead.*

Segno (Sign)
*A musical marker that denotes a point
in the music that will be revisted later.*

Coda
*Designates the start a section of music
that prolongs the end of the peice.*

Mesure Repeat
*Shorthand symbol used to repeat
the previous measure of music.*

Fermata
*Indicates that the note below should
be played slightly longer than normal*

D.C./D.S.

D.C. and D.S. markers
*Marks the point of return to the to the beginning
of the piece (D.C.) or a return to the Segno (D.S)*

al Coda/ al Fine

"al Coda" and "al Fine" Markers
*Used with D.C and D.S markers, indicates for the
performer to play to the end of the peice (al Fine)
or to the start of the Coda (al Coda)*

CHAPTER 2 - OPEN POSITION NOTES

The **Open Position** is the first position that we will learn to read notes on the guitar as it incorporates the open strings plus the first four frets of the guitar. This position is used to read in the lowest register of the guitar as it adds the low E, F, and G that are not found in any other position.

The goal of this chapter is to memorize the locations of the notes in open position in the diagram below, by matching the note to the tablature location directly below. It is best to memorize one string at a time

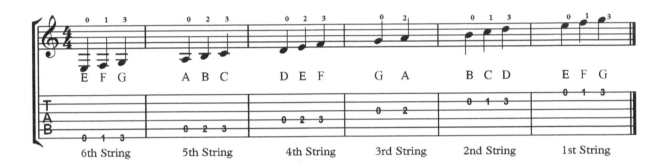

Practice the following exercises to learn the note locations on each string.

Open Position Reading Examples

Excerpt from "Invention No. 1 in C Major" by.: J.S Bach

Excerpt from "Prelude in C Major" by: J.S Bach

Excerpt from "Orchestral Suite #3" by: J.S Bach

Sharps and Flats

♯

Sharp
Raises a note by one half step (one fret)

♭

Flat
Lowers a note by one half step (one fret)

Notes can be altered (raised or lowered in pitch) using symbols called *Sharps* and *Flats*. A sharp raises a note up a half-step (the distance of one fret) while a flat will lower a note one half step. **Sharps and flats lower or raise the note for the duration of the measure.**

In the next measure, the note returns to its natural sound. Notes can either be spelled with a Sharp or a Flat, which means that F# and Gb are the same note. Therefore a Sharp or Flat can look different in standard notation even though it is played in the same position on the guitar.

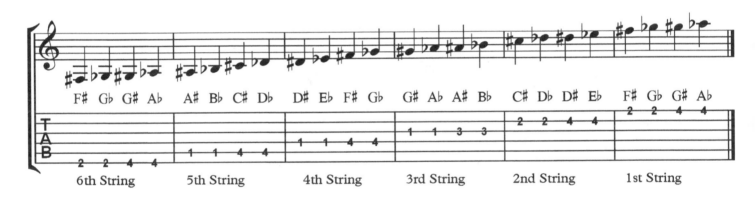

Excerpt from "Cello Prelude Suite No. 1" by: J.S Bach - Key of D

Excerpt from "Cello Prelude Suite No. 1" by: J.S Bach - Key of Bb

Keys and The Major Scale

The Major Scale is the "D.N.A" of music. All of the chords, key signatures and musical examples we have seen earlier in the book and will learn later are derived from the major scale. This chapter will help you understand how the major scale is constructed and how to use them in music.

All scales are made up of *intervals*. In order to get the sound of a particular scale or chord, we must use a certain type of interval in a specific order. The first two kinds of intervals we are going to talk about are HALF STEPS and WHOLE STEPS. A half step is the interval equal to the distance of one fret. As an example, if we play the 1st fret to the 2nd fret on the low E string, we would be moving from F to F#, which is the distance of a half step.

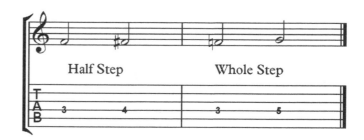

A whole step is the interval equal to the distance of two frets. A whole step up would be playing the 1st fret to the 3rd fret on the low E string and moving from F to G.

Combining Whole Steps and Half Steps: The C Major Scale

When we combine the use of whole steps and half steps, we create scales. The formula for a major scale is: **Whole Step- Whole Step - Half Step -Whole Step - Whole Step - Whole Step - Half Step.** The basis for western music theory is the combination of whole and half steps known as the MAJOR SCALE. By starting on a root note and following this formula, we can find the notes in any major scale.

Observe the C Major Scale below with the Whole and Half Steps.

Notice the difference in the G Major Scale below with the Whole and Half Steps. Note that the F# was added to complete the formula, as the distance between E and F is a half-step.

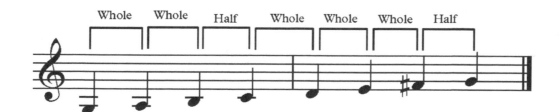

Key Signatures

As we learned with the Major Scale, using sharps and flats can alter the key of a song. In certain keys, certain sharps and flats are used frequently. In order to determine the key of a piece of music, and to save the composer from writing each sharp and flat in the music, a *KEY SIGNATURE* is used to automatically raise or lower certain notes in the song.

Sharp Keys

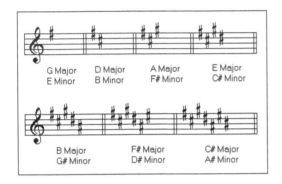

Flat Keys

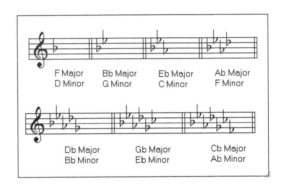

Excerpt from "Cello Prelude Suite No. 1" by: J.S Bach - Key of D

Excerpt from "Cello Prelude Suite No. 1" by: J.S Bach - Key of D with Key Signature

Natural Signs

When a key signature is used, it alters the pitches for the entire piece of music. To return to the "natural" or unaltered note, a *NATURAL SIGN* cancels out a previously written sharp or flat until another sharp or flat is written or the measure ends.

♮

Natural Sign
*Cancels out a previously written sharp or flat
until another sharp or flat is written or the measure ends.*

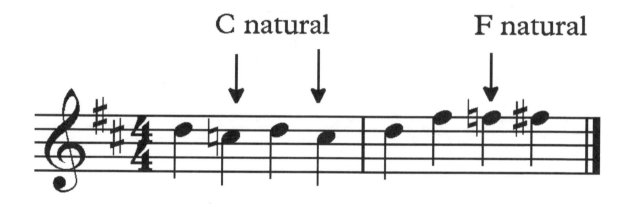

Excerpt from "Invention No. 4" by: J.S Bach

Excerpt from "Invention No. 2" by: J.S Bach

CHAPTER 2 APPENDIX- OPEN POSITION SONGS

"Liverpool Melody"

"Sit Next To Me"

"What Can Make Me Feel This Way?"

"Surf Music USA"

"All The Lonely People"

"Walkin Into Memphis"

"Surf Music USA"

"The King of Graceland"

CHAPTER 3 - OPEN CHORDS

Major Chords

A *Chord* is a group of three or more notes played at the same time. A Major chord is the combination of a Root note, (usually the lowest note of the chord), the 3rd, and the 5th. As you see in the diagram below, if we start with the note C as our root, the 3rd would be two notes above the root, which is the note E. The fifth is found two notes above the third, which is the note G. This combination gives us the notes of a C Major chord. Major Chords are characterized by a bright, happy sound.

In a Major Chord, the distance between the Root and the 3rd is known as a Major 3rd (M3) and the distance between the 3rd and 5th is known as a Minor 3rd (m3).

Minor Chords

Like a Major chord, a *Minor Chord* contains a Root, 3rd and 5th. Unlike the major chord, the 3rd of a minor chord is lowered by one fret, giving the chord a darker, sadder sound. The 3rd of the chord (E) is lowered to an E flat, creating a C minor chord.

Note the lowered 3rd of the minor chord. Also note that the Minor 3rd is now between the root and 3rd, while the Major 3rd is between the 3rd and 5th.

Playing Major and Minor Chords On the Guitar

Play each note of the chord so that you can hear each note of the chord. If you cannot hear one of the notes, check for these two things:

1. ***Make sure that your fingers are not touching other strings:*** If a finger blocks another string, you will not hear that note in the chord.

2. ***Press down hard on each note of the chord***: Applying more pressure with your fingers will result in a better sounding chord.

The first chords we will learn are the ***A major***, ***A minor***, ***E major***, and ***E minor*** chords

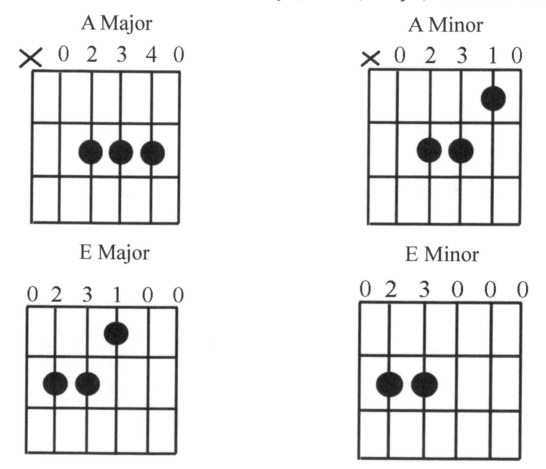

Moving Between Chords

Now that we have learned the shapes and notes of our first four chords, we need to learn how to switch between one chord and the next. Try to visualize the next chord while you are playing the first chord. Just as a driver looks ahead to watch for traffic hazards, a guitarist must look ahead to the next chord they are playing. Use your eyes to guide each finger to the next chord *before* switching the chord.

Chord Switching Exercises

Exercise 1

Exercise 2

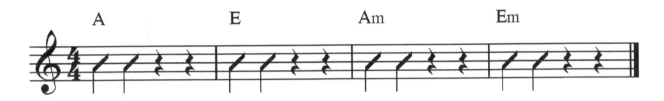

Exercise 3

Exercise 4

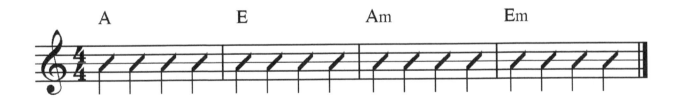

The next chords we will learn are the *C major*, *G major*, *D major*, and *D minor* chords

C Major

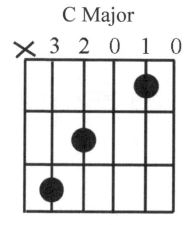

G Major

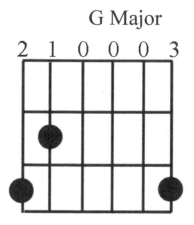

D Major

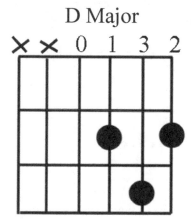

D Minor

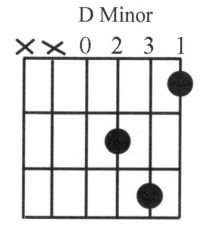

Exercise 1

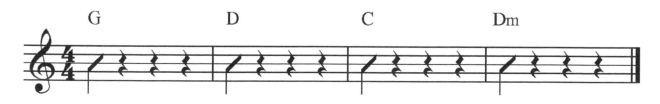

Exercise 2

Exercise 3

Exercise 4

Chord Review Exercises

Exercise 1

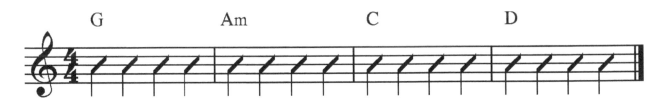

Exercise 2

Dominant 7th Chords

By adding the 7th degree of the scale to a major chord, we can create *Dominant 7th* chords. 7th chords create a very unique sound that is often found in blues, country, classical, and jazz music.

E7
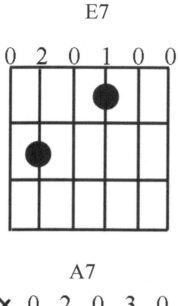

C7
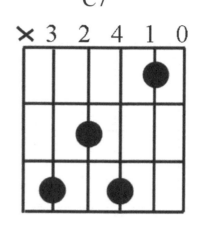

A7
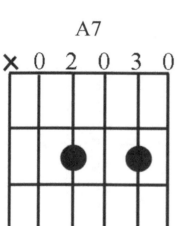

D7
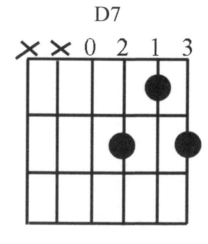

B7
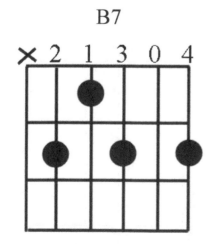

G7
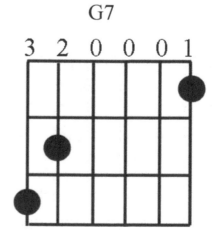

Dominant 7th Chord Exercises

Exercise 1

Exercise 2

Exercise 3

Exercise 4

Inversions and Altered Bass Chords

An *Inversion* is a chord that has a note other than the root of that chord as its lowest note. A *First Inversion* chord has the *3rd* of the chord in the bass and a *Second Inversion* chord has the 5th of the chord as the lowest note. Occasionally a chord will have a *Non-Chord Tone* as its lowest note, and this is simply called an *Altered Bass Chord*.

Inversions and Altered Bass chords are noted by the following chord symbol. The letter before the backslash determines the chord, while the letter to the right of the backslash denotes the bass note of that chord.

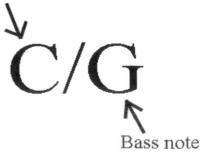

Name of the chord played

Bass note

Chord Inversions

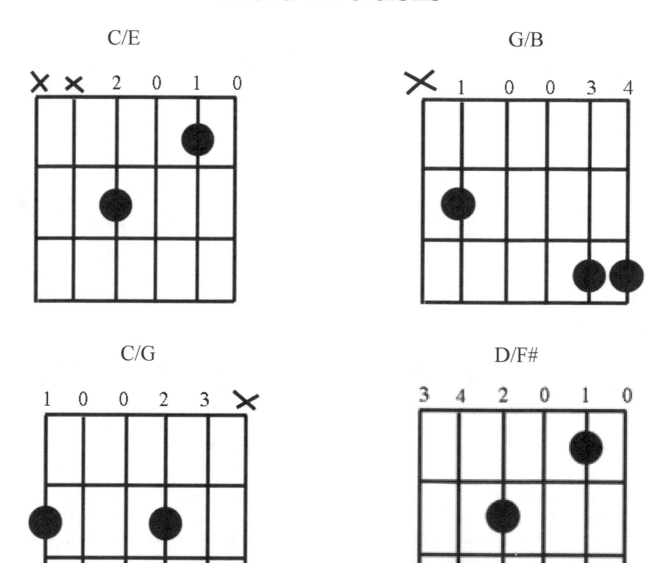

Chord Inversion Exercises

Exercise 1

Exercise 2

Exercise 3

Exercise 4

The F Major Chord

The F major chord requires two notes to be played with the index finger. This is our first introduction to BARRE chords which require a flattened index finger to stretch across the top two strings to play both notes on the 1st fret. This will require some practice as it will be difficult to make every note ring correctly at first.

F Major

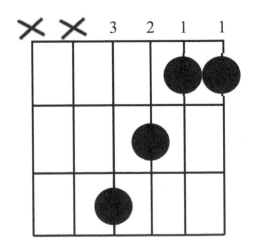

Open Chord Review

Exercise 1

Exercise 2

Exercise 3

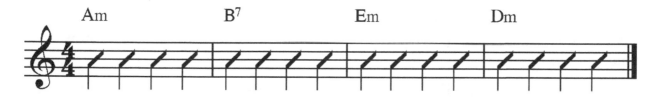

Exercise 4

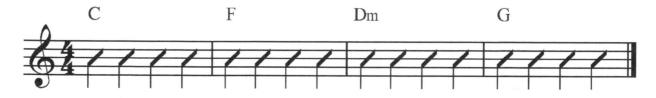

Exercise 5

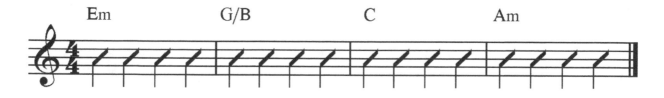

CHAPTER 4 - STRUMMING PATTERNS

Now that we have learned some open chord shapes, we need to learn how to strum each of these chords. Learning how to strum chords will allow us to play several songs using the open chords that we learned in the last chapter.

Rhythmic Notation

When writing chords, sometimes its easier to write the rhythms and chord symbols rather than each note in the chord. For this type of notation, we use variations of our pitched notes called **Rhythmic Notation** to write out the rhythms played without writing exact pitches.

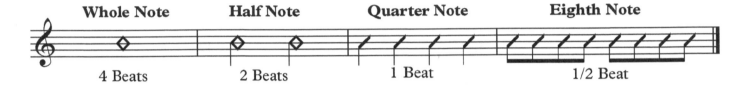

Basics of Strumming

There are some basic rules to understand before learning to strum patterns on the guitar: Downbeats are played by strumming down towards the ground, while Upbeats are strummed upward towards the sky (this is similar to how we played quarter and eighth notes in chapter 1). This allows our hand to work like a pendulum, strumming the guitar twice for each downward motion.

Notice how each quarter note is strummed using a downstroke. When we add the eighth notes, the downbeats are still strummed using downstrokes while the upbeats are strummed using an upstroke.

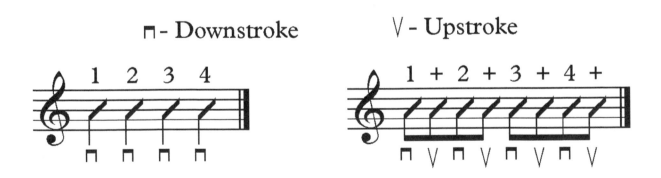

Any strummed note that falls on a **downbeat** will be played as a **downstroke**, and anything falling on the **upbeats** (on the "+") will be played as an **upstroke**. This is a rule we will always follow no matter how complex the strumming pattern or combination of notes.

See the examples below for different strumming pattern rhythms.

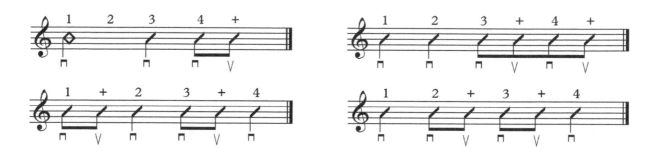

Rhythmic Notation Examples

Now that we understand the basics of strumming and rhythmic notation, practice the following rhythms using any chord. Try to read ahead so that the changes in the patterns do not catch you by surprise.

Exercise 1

Exercise 2

Exercise 3

Exercise 4

Strumming Pattern Exercises

Here are some more exercises to get you more comfortable strumming on the guitar. Pick any open chord that you want to play while working on these patterns so you can hear what they sound like. Repeat each pattern several times until you feel comfortable enough to play it through at least 4 consecutive times.

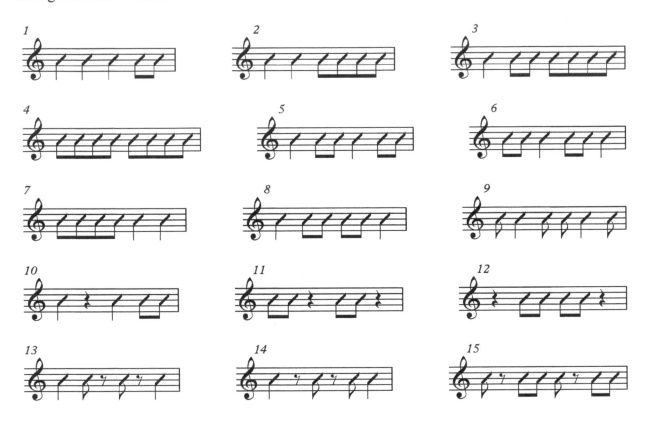

Strumming Patterns Using Ties

Sometimes songs use strumming patterns that do not always strum each beat. In order to notate this, a mark called a *Tie* is used. A *Tie* connects two notes so that when the first note is strummed, it is held for the duration of the original note as well as the tied note.

Ties can also be used to hold notes across a barline into the next measure.

Strumming Pattern Exercises Using Ties

Here are some more exercises to get you more comfortable strumming on the guitar. Pick any open chord that you want to play while working on these patterns so you can hear what they sound like. Repeat each pattern several times until you feel comfortable enough to play it through at least 4 consecutive times. Be sure to write the patterns underneath the exercises to help you.

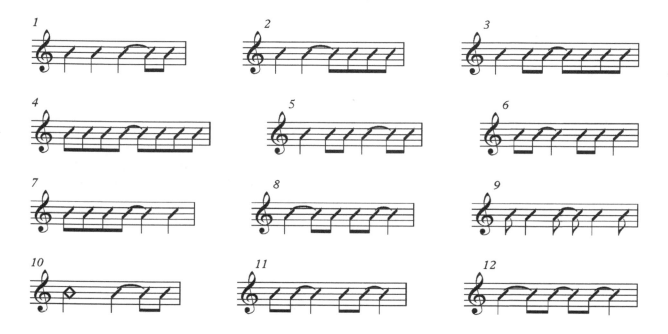

Two-Measure Strumming Pattern Exercises

Here are some more exercises to get you more comfortable strumming on the guitar. Pick any open chord that you want to play while working on these patterns so you can hear what they sound like. Repeat each pattern several times until you feel comfortable enough to play it through at least 4 consecutive times.

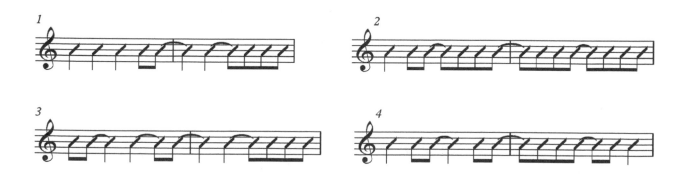

Combining Chords and Strumming Patterns

Now that we have learned both open chords and how to strum the guitar, we can start to learn some songs that combine a chord progression with a strumming pattern. Practice each of these songs slowly, as it will be difficult at first to synchronize your right and left hand. Practice the chord progression without the strumming pattern (similar to the open chord exercises in chapter 2) and then gradually add the strumming pattern in beat by beat as you get more comfortable with the chords.

Exercise 1

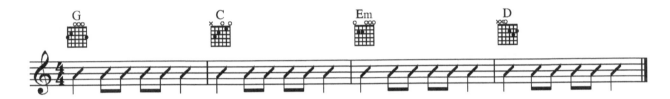

Exercise 2

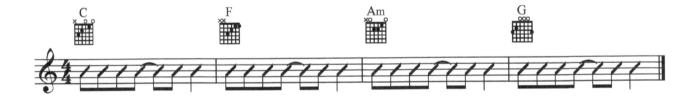

Exercise 3

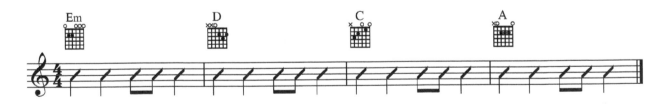

Exercise 4

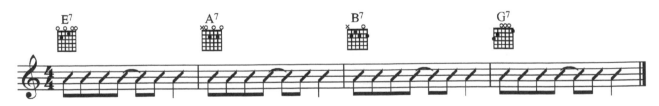

Strumming Study #1
Whole, Half, Quarter and Eigth Notes

Strumming Study #2

Notes and Rests

Strumming Study #3

Notes, and Ties

Copyright © 2012 Donovan Raitt

CHAPTER 4 APPENDIX- CHORDS AND STRUMMING SONGS

"Liverpool Melody"

"Sit Next To Me"

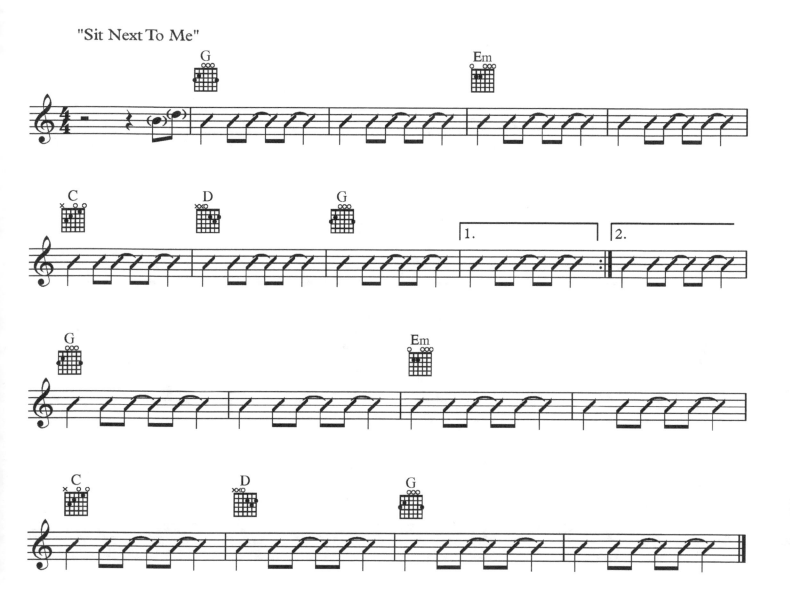

"Surf Music USA"

"All The Lonely People"

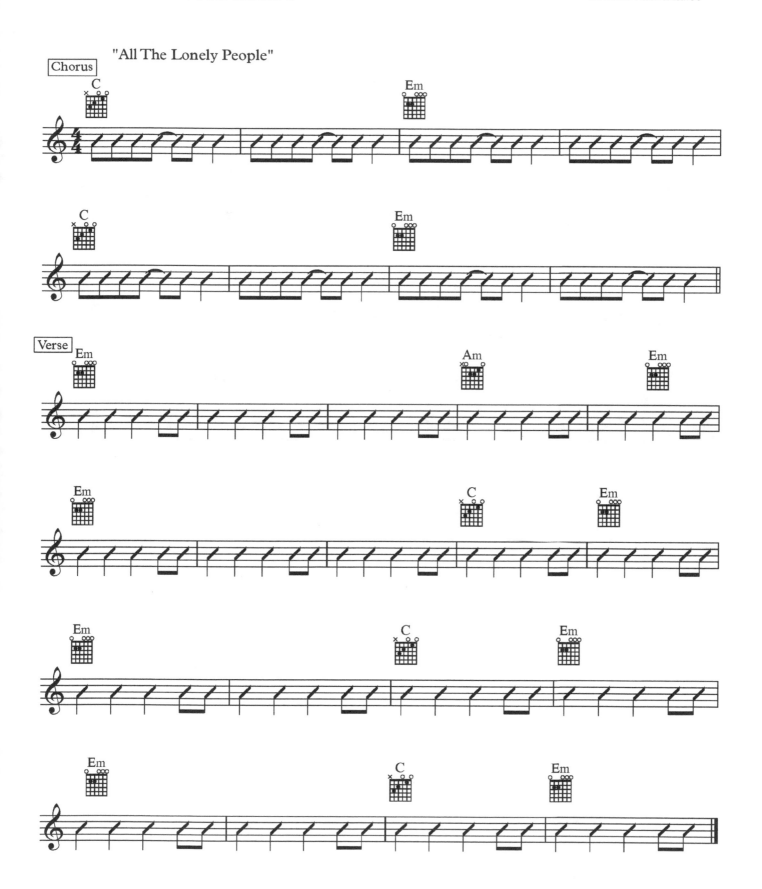

"The King of Graceland"

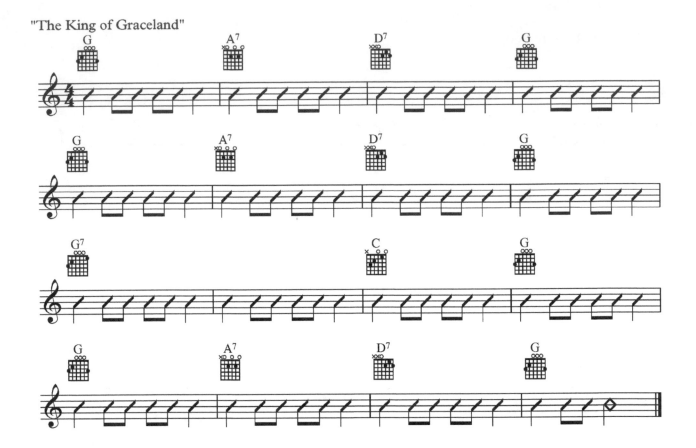

"What Can Make Me Feel This Way?"

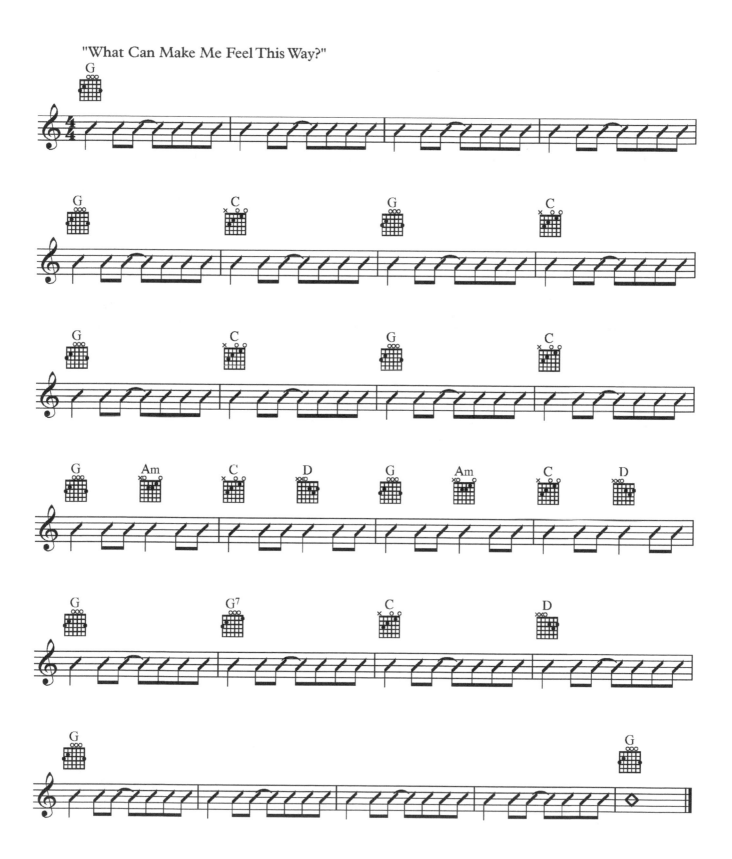

"Walkin Into Memphis"

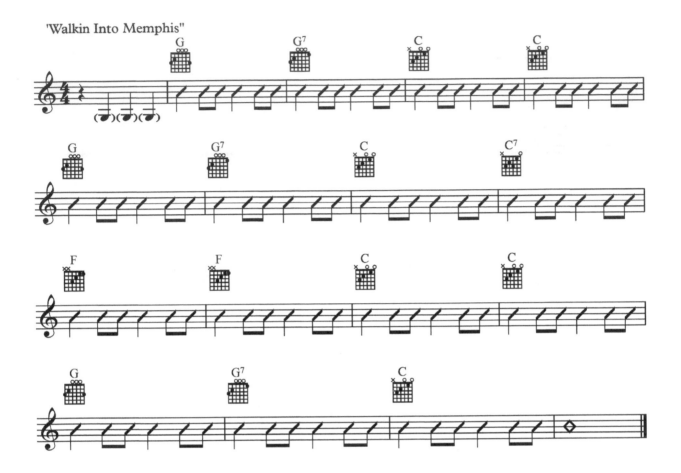

CHAPTER 5 - POWER CHORDS

The "Power Chord" is one of the most common chords used in rock music. The power chord is simply a two-note chord, consisting of the root note and the note a 5th above the root. This combination of two notes creates a very powerful sound on the guitar, especially when distortion is used.

The power chord is neither major nor minor, because it does not contain the note a 3rd above the root (in Chapter 2, we learned that the 3rd of the chord determines whether the chord is major or minor). This allows the same chord shape to be played to imply both major and minor harmonies.

The "Power Chord" can be moved up and down on the guitar to create different chords with the same shape. This allows the guitarist to use it frequently and quickly. By placing our first finger on the correct root note, we will create a power chord with that root. Use the two diagrams below to find the correct root and play the examples on the next few pages.

Power Chord Shape with an E String" Root

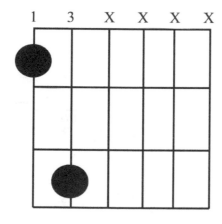

Power Chord Shape with an A String" Root

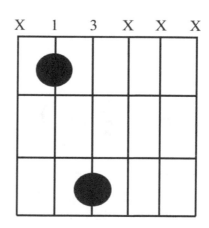

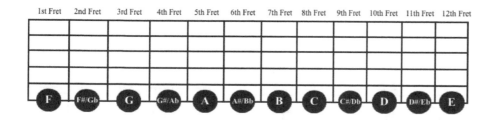

Root notes on the 6th (E) String

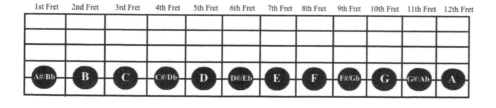

Root notes on the 5th (A) String

Power Chord Exercises

Practice the following exercises using "power chords" instead of normal open chords. Be careful not to strum other strings while playing these chords. You can use your first and third fingers to mute the other strings if needed.

Exercise 1

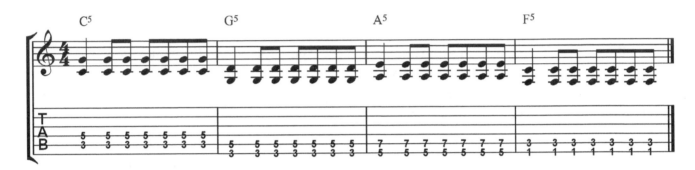

Exercise 2

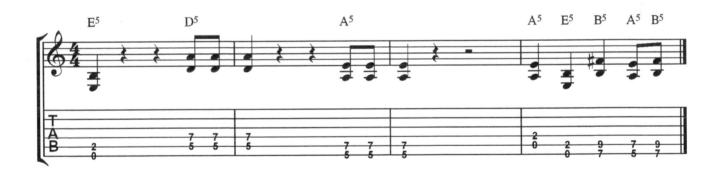

Exercise 3

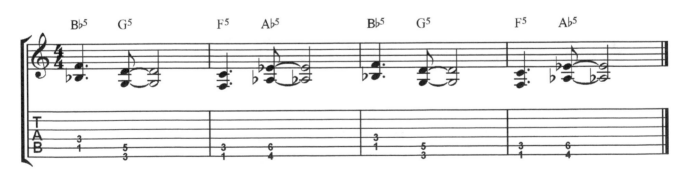

CHAPTER 6 - BARRE CHORDS AND THE CAGED SYSTEM

By placing our index finger across the strings behind an open chord shape, we can change the pitches of the open strings and transpose the chord to play a *Barre Chord*. Barre Chords are extremely challenging to play at first, as they require a lot of strength to bar across the guitar neck while pressing down on the chord shapes.

Five tips on how to play Barre chords:

1. Make sure to keep your thumb behind your first finger. Place your thumb directly behind the lower part of your first finger.

2. Use the side of your 1st finger to barre across the fret to get an even sound on all six strings.

3. Press down with a lot of pressure on each string.

4. Play one string at a time to hear each string instead of strumming the chord.

5. Never use your fingertip. It should be resting slightly above the guitar neck

The CAGED System

The CAGED System is an acronym for the chord shapes that can be transposed to barre chords (C, A, G, E, and D chords) For example, and E major chord can be moved up 2 frets to play an F# Chord by placing a bar on the second fret and playing an E major chord shape in front of the bar as if it were an open chord. By changing the root of the chord, we can change the sound of the chord. This allows us to play many chords that cannot be played as open chords on the guitar.

How to Find Any Major or Minor Chord Using the CAGED System

• **Find the root of the CAGED shape:** E and G shapes have their root on the Low E (6th) string. A and C Shapes have their root on the A (5th) string, and D shapes have their roots on the D (4th) String.

• **Use the root diagrams** to find the new root of the transposed chord shape and place the root there to create the chord in the new key.

• **Adjust the fingering** of the voicing to free up your index finger to create the barre.

CAGED System - Finding the Roots

In order to use the CAGED system, we will need to find the correct root for each chord. Use the following fretboard diagrams to find the root for the chord you are looking for. Remember that the E, A, and D shapes will have the root as part of the barre, while the C and G shapes use a fretting finger for the root. For example, if you want to play an F# chord using an E Major Shape, find the F# on the 2nd fret of the Low E (6th) string and place the barre on the 2nd fret. Then add the E major shape in front of it to complete the chord.

Root notes on the Low E (6th) String

1st Fret	2nd Fret	3rd Fret	4th Fret	5th Fret	6th Fret	7th Fret	8th Fret	9th Fret	10th Fret	11th Fret	12th Fret
F	F#/Gb	G	G#/Ab	A	A#/Bb	B	C	C#/Db	D	D#/Eb	E

Root notes on the A (5th) String

1st Fret	2nd Fret	3rd Fret	4th Fret	5th Fret	6th Fret	7th Fret	8th Fret	9th Fret	10th Fret	11th Fret	12th Fret
A#/Bb	B	C	C#/Db	D	D#/Eb	E	F	F#/Gb	G	G#/Ab	A

Root notes on the D (4th) String

1st Fret	2nd Fret	3rd Fret	4th Fret	5th Fret	6th Fret	7th Fret	8th Fret	9th Fret	10th Fret	11th Fret	12th Fret
D#/Eb	E	F	F#/Gb	G	G#/Ab	A	A#/Bb	B	C	C#/Db	D

CAGED System Chord Shapes

E Major Shape

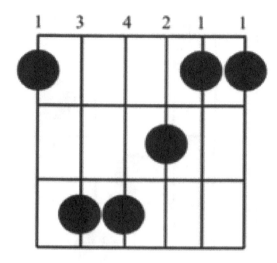

E Minor Shape

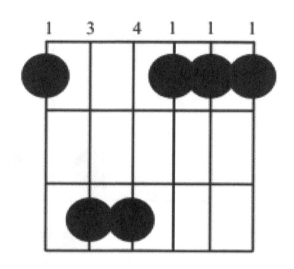

A Major Shape

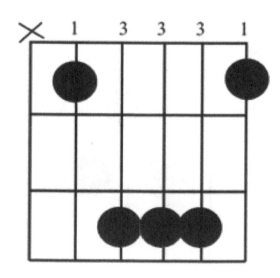

A Minor Shape

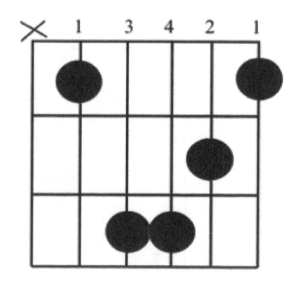

D Major Shape

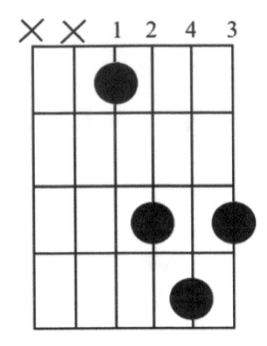

D Minor Shape

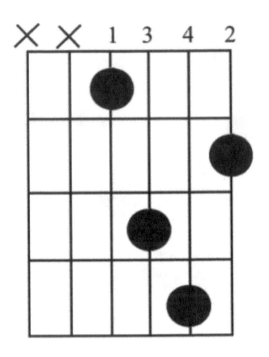

C Major Shape

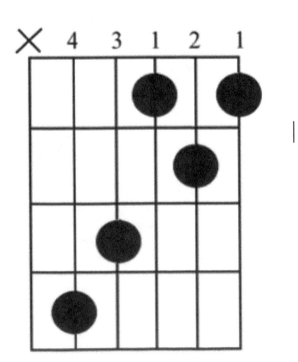

C Minor Shape

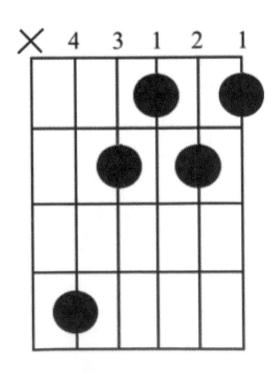

G Major Shape

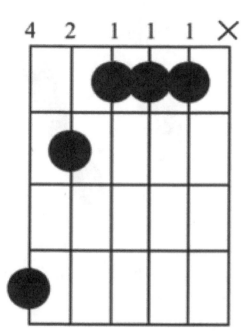

G Minor Shape

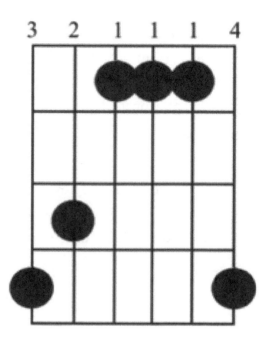

CAGED System Exercises

Play the following exercises by finding the chord shapes using the CAGED system. Be sure to find the chords using multiple shapes to better understand how the CAGED system works.

Exercise 1

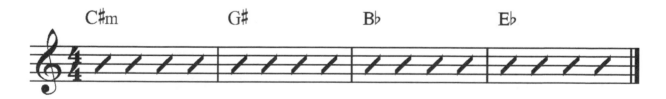

Exercise 2

Using a Capo with the CAGED System

A "Capo" is a device used by guitarists to change the tuning of the open strings to play in different keys using familiar chord shapes. The term "Capo" is short for the Italian *Capo Tasto* (Capo = *Head*, Tasto = *Tie, or Fret*), and was first used by 17th century guitarists. The capo is a very useful tool for guitarists who prefer to play open chords in different keys without retuning the guitar.

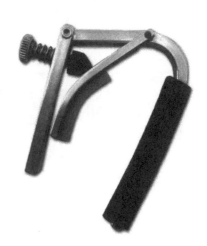

The Capo can be used in conjunction with the CAGED system to play open chords in any key by placing the capo on the appropriate fret. The table below shows where to place the capo for all 12 keys and for the 5 CAGED shapes.

For example: if you want to transpose a song from the key of C major to the key of E major, you can place the capo on the 4th fret and play a C shape for the E major chord.

Key	C Shape	A Shape	G Shape	E Shape	D Shape
C	Open	3rd Fret	5th Fret	8th Fret	10th Fret
C#/Db	1st Fret	4th Fret	6th Fret	9th Fret	11th Fret
D	2nd Fret	5th Fret	7th Fret	10th Fret	Open
D#/Eb	3rd Fret	6th Fret	8th Fret	11th Fret	1st Fret
E	4th Fret	7th Fret	9th Fret	Open	2nd Fret
F	5th Fret	8th Fret	10th Fret	1st Fret	3rd Fret
F#/Gb	6th Fret	9th Fret	11th Fret	2nd Fret	4th Fret
G	7th Fret	10th Fret	Open	3rd Fret	5th Fret
G#/Ab	8th Fret	11th Fret	1st Fret	4th Fret	6th Fret
A	9th Fret	Open	2nd Fret	5th Fret	7th Fret
A#/Bb	10th Fret	1st Fret	3rd Fret	6th Fret	8th Fret
B	11th Fret	2nd Fret	4th Fret	7th Fret	9th Fret

CHAPTER 7 - 5TH POSITION READING

Since the guitar has six strings, most notes on the guitar can be found in several "positions" on the fretboard. Instead of learning all of the note locations at once, we can divide the guitar into positions to help us locate the best fingering for each piece of music. We can determine the best position by studying the range (highest and lowest note) of the piece to find a suitable position

The "5th Position" refers to the notes found between the 5th and 8th frets on the guitar. This is the most versatile position on the neck, as you can play into both the lower and upper ranges of the guitar. Note that this position goes up to the High C as well as the Low A, and is the most balanced range for reading into the low and high notes.

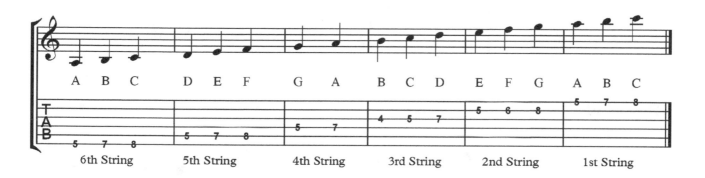

The diagram above shows the notes in the 5th position as well as their positions on the fretboard.

Excerpt from "Caprice #2" - Nicolo Paganini

Excerpt from "Orchestral Suite #3" by: J.S Bach

Reading Chords and Multiple Notes

Part of reading on the guitar involves reading multiple notes at the same time. Very often you will have to read chords in addition to single note lines. Read the examples below and find the best fingering for each chord. You may find many of these examples similar to the open chords you learned in previous chapters.

Exercise 1

Exercise 2

Exercise 3

Exercise 4

CHAPTER 8 - TRIADS AND INVERSIONS

In chapter 3, we learned open chords and in chapter 5 we learned about moving open chord shapes to create new chords using the **CAGED system** and **Barre Chords**. As we develop our chord knowledge, it's important to be able to play smaller versions of the chords we've learned, as guitar chord voicings can include multiples of the same note.

Triad voicings contain one of each of the notes required to play a major or minor chord, and create a more concise and focused sound than open or barre chords. In this chapter we will learn triad shapes for all four string sets, so you can break down larger CAGED shapes into simple triads.

Root Position

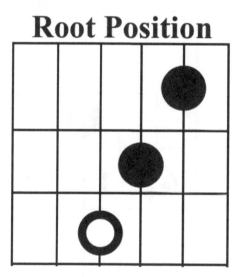

1st Inversion

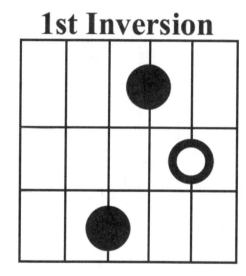

2nd Inversion

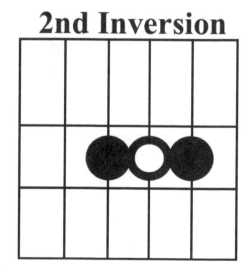

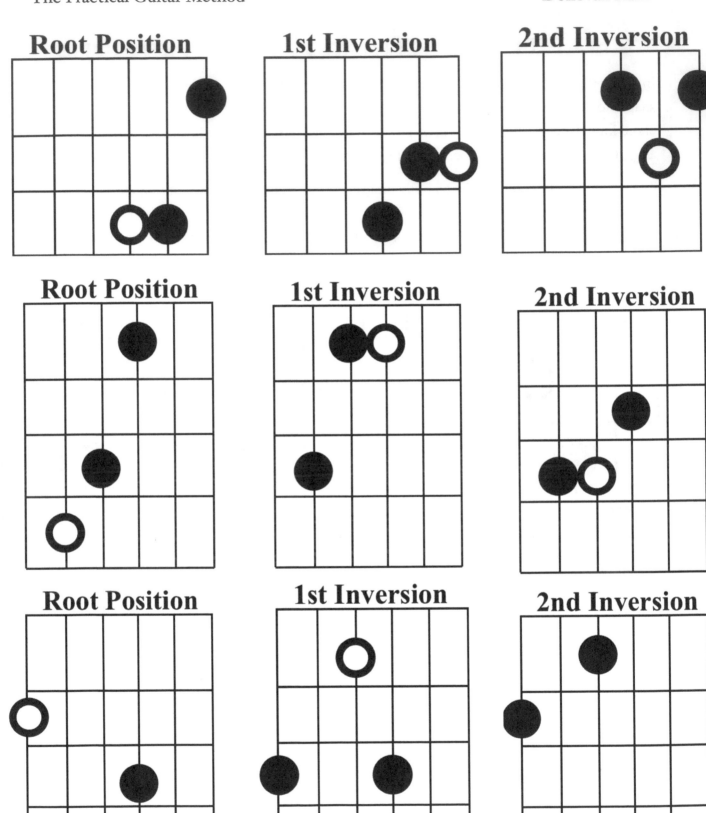

Triads and Inversions Exercises

Practice the following exercise using the triad shapes above. Make sure to practice each set separately as to learn how to move each string set across the fretboard.

CHAPTER 9 - 16TH NOTE STRUMMING

16th notes can be used to create faster, more percussive attacks on the guitar and allow us to keep the pulse of the song moving faster. 16th notes are strummed just like 8th notes, however for every two 8th notes there are four 16th notes, so our strumming will have to be quicker as a result.

Notice how each eight note is now strummed using a downstroke. When we add the 16th notes, the downbeats are still strummed using downstrokes while the upbeats are strummed using an upstroke.

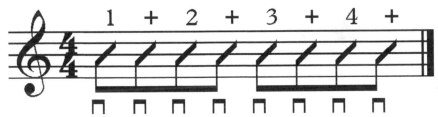

Notice how the 8th notes are now all strummed using *downstrokes*. This is only the case when 16th notes are present in the strumming pattern

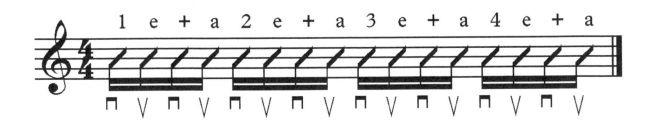

With 16th notes, we now have four strums in the space of one quarter note. We count these groups of 16th notes as *"One -E And-A, Two-E-And-Uh..."* and so on for each beat.

Remember: Any strummed note that falls on a *downbeat* will be played as a *downstroke,* and anything falling in-between downbeats will be played as an *upstroke*. We are simply changing the upstrokes from the quarter notes as seen before to the 8th notes.

Strumming Patterns with 16th Notes

Here are some more exercises to get you more comfortable strumming 16th note patterns. Pick any chord that you want to play (don't forget barre chords!) while working on these patterns so you can hear what they sound like. Repeat each pattern several times until you feel comfortable enough to play it through at least 4 consecutive times.

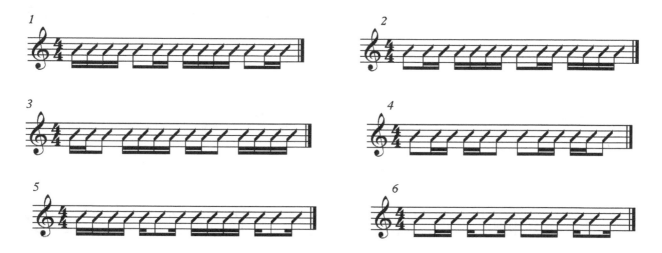

16th Note Rests and Single 16th notes

Just like with other types of notes we have studied, 16th notes also have rests, that look very similar to 8th rests with an additional flag on the stem. Practice these examples to get used to 16th notes and 16th rests.

It is important to make sure that you are using the correct picking directions, so write in the strumming patterns before you play each pattern. Start at a slow tempo before moving up to faster tempos as 16th notes will be much faster than 8th notes at slower tempos.

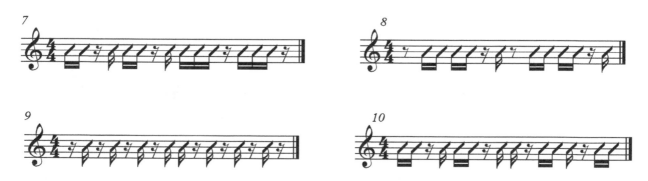

Strumming Study #4

Sixteenth Notes

Strumming Study #5

Sixteenth Notes and Ties

Strumming Study #6
Dotted Rhythms

CHAPTER 10 - MAJOR AND MINOR SCALES

Scales are the building blocks of music. All of the chords, key signatures and musical examples we have seen earlier in the book are derived from some type of scale. This chapter will help you understand how scales are constructed and how to use them in music.

All scales are made up of *intervals*. In order to get the sound of a particular scale or chord, we must use a certain type of interval in a specific order. The first two kinds of intervals we are going to talk about are HALF STEPS and WHOLE STEPS. A half step is the interval equal to the distance of one fret. As an example, if we play the 1st fret to the 2nd fret on the low E string, we would be moving from F to F#, which is the distance of a half step.

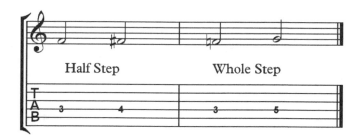

A whole step is the interval equal to the distance of two frets. A whole step up would be playing the 1st fret to the 3rd fret on the low E string and moving from F to G.

Combining Whole Steps and Half Steps: The C Major Scale

When we combine the use of whole steps and half steps, we create scales. The formula for a major scale is: **Whole Step- Whole Step - Half Step -Whole Step - Whole Step - Whole Step - Half Step.** The basis for western music theory is the combination of whole and half steps known as the MAJOR SCALE. By starting on a root note and following this formula, we can find the notes in any major scale.

Observe the C Major Scale below with the Whole and Half Steps.

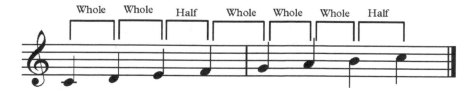

Notice the difference in the G Major Scale below with the Whole and Half Steps. Note that the F# was added to complete the formula, as the distance between E and F is a half-step.

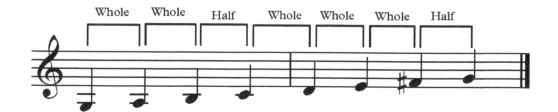

Donovan Raitt

C Major Scale - 1st Position (E Shape)

2nd Position (D Shape)

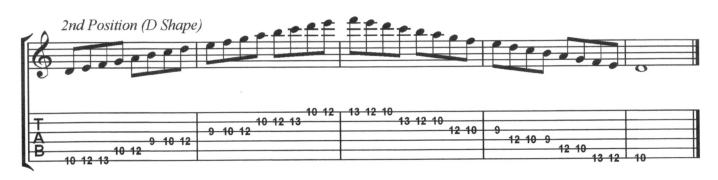

3rd Position (C Shape)

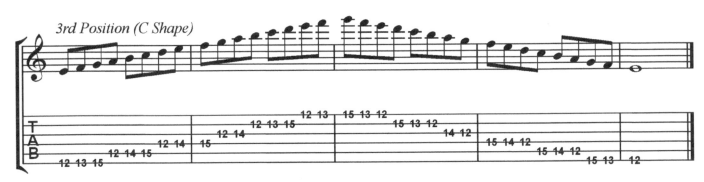

4th Position (A Shape)

5th Position (G Shape)

1st Position

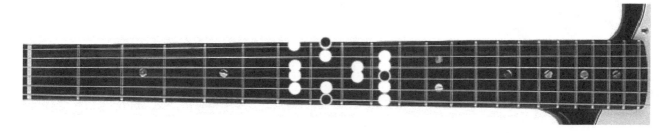

2nd Position

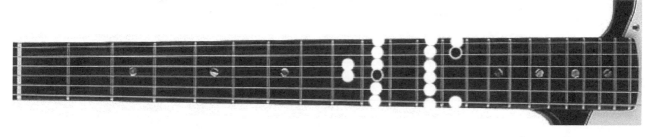

3rd Position

4th Position

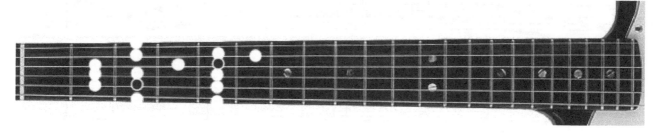

5th Position

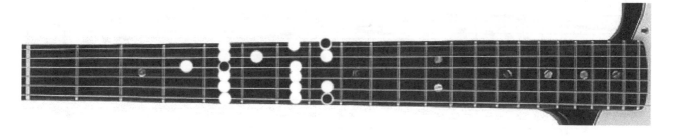

1st Position

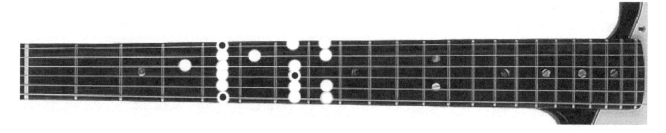

2nd Position

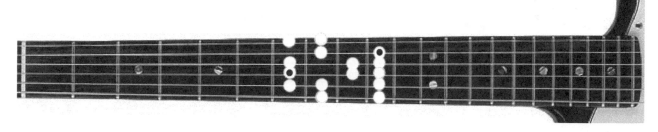

3rd Position

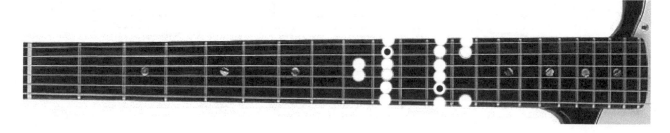

4th Position

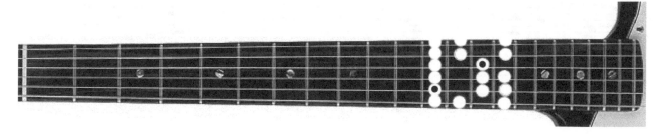

5th Position

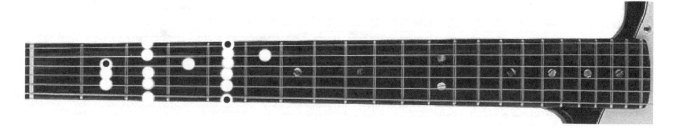

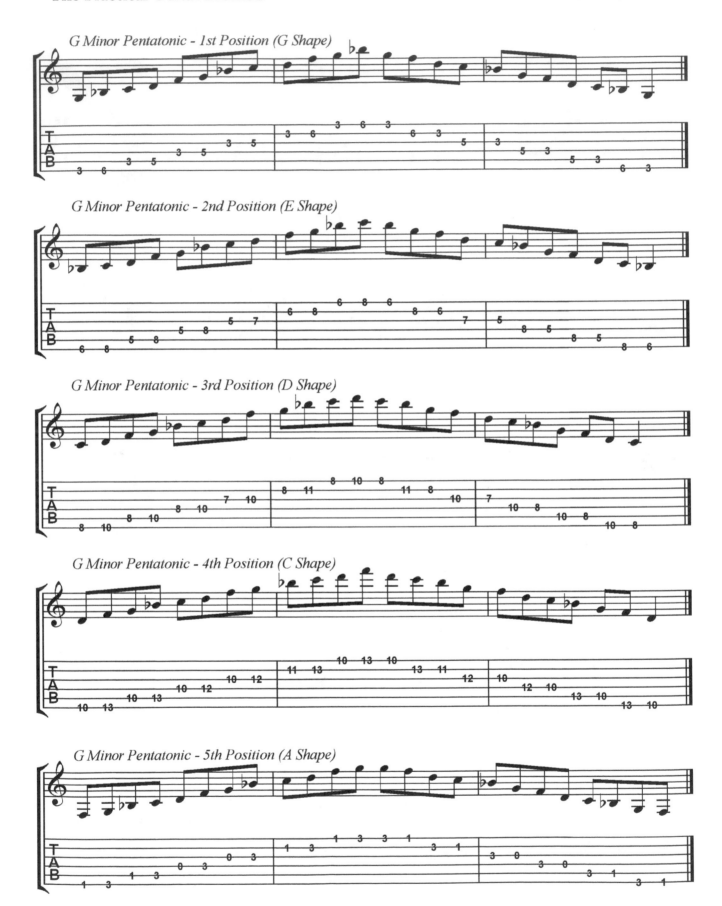

Minor Scales - Relative and Parallel Minor

There are four types of minor scales that we need to learn in this chapter. The two most common types of minor scales are the PARALLEL MINOR and the RELATIVE MINOR.

The Parallel Minor

The parallel minor key is a minor key that shares the same root, but not the same notes with a major key. The key of G minor is the parallel minor key of G major, because although they share the same root note, they contain different notes.

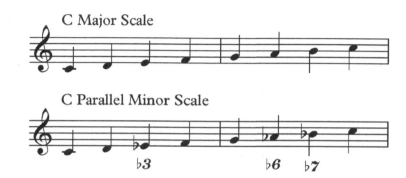

The Relative Minor: The A Minor Scale

Each major scale has a relative minor scale, which uses the same notes as its relative major scale. The relative minor starts on the 6th degree of a major scale. For example, in the key of C, the relative minor scale starts on the 6th note from the root, which is the note A. Notice that both scales have the exact same notes but start with different roots.

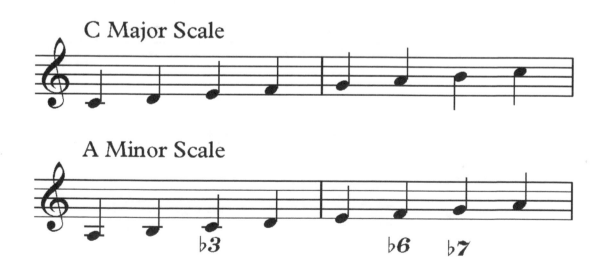

Other Types of Minor Scales

The Harmonic Minor Scale

The harmonic minor scale is a minor scale with a raised 7th degree. This scale includes the leading tone from the parallel major scale (A major) in order to produce the leading tone of the major scale in the minor scale

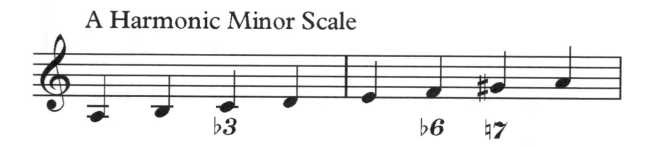

The Melodic Minor Scale

The melodic minor scale adds the raised 6th degree to the harmonic minor to create more of the parallel major sound (A major) in a minor key. This is also known as a hybrid major/minor scale. Note that this scale is only played ascending and reverts to the natural minor descending

The Pentatonic Scale

The pentatonic scale is a five-note scale (*penta=five tonic=notes*) that is similar in sound to the major and minor seven note scales. The pentatonic scale was originally found in Japanese music, and was adapted into western music by 19th century French impressionist composers Claude Debussy and Maurice Ravel. Since its introduction, the pentatonic scale has been found most frequently in rock and blues music, because of its unique and distinctive sound.

The Major Pentatonic Scale

The formula for the *Major Pentatonic Scale* omits the 4th and 7th from the major scale, and leaves the Root, 2nd, 3rd, 5th, and 6th degrees of the major scale.

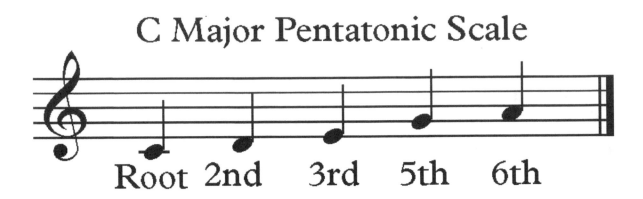

The Minor Pentatonic Scale

The formula for the *Minor Pentatonic Scale* omits the 2nd and 6th from the major scale, and leaves the Root, b3rd, 4th 5th, and b7th degrees of the minor scale.

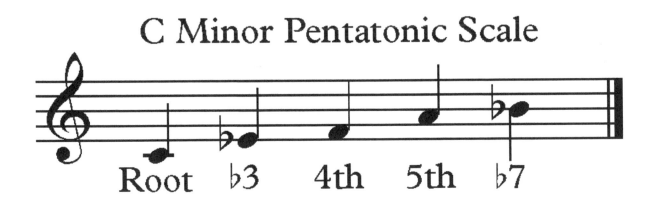

The pentatonic scale utilizes the same position system as the major and minor scales. On the next page we will see the five positions for the pentatonic scales in the key of G minor and Bb major (since they are relative keys they share the same notes).

1st Position

2nd Position

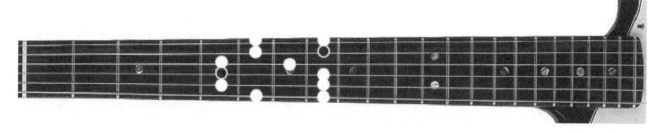

3rd Position

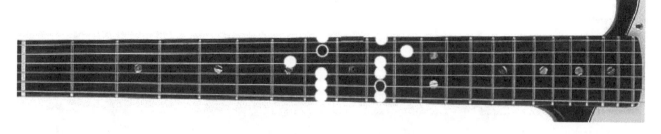

4th Position

5th Position

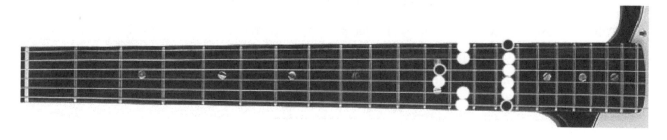

CHAPTER 11 - PALM MUTING

Palm muting is a very important technique in the development of your guitar playing. By placing your palm across the strings on the bridge of the guitar, you can mute the strings and get a tight, muted sound. To be clear, you are not "muting" the strings so there is no pitch, but "dampening" the strings so there is no sustain to the string once it is plucked.

Hand Placement

In order to correctly mute the strings, you must place the back of your palm directly across the bridge. You want to put your hand right where the strings touch the bridge so that your hand touches both the strings and the bridge. From this point, use your palm as a pivot point to strum the strings.

As you move down the guitar, move your hand so that you have enough pressure on the higher strings of the guitar as well. You should be able to hear each note clearly, if your hand is too far away from the bridge, you will not hear the notes. If your hand is too far back, the notes will not sound muted. Find the spot on your guitar where this feels comfortable, as it will be different on each guitar.

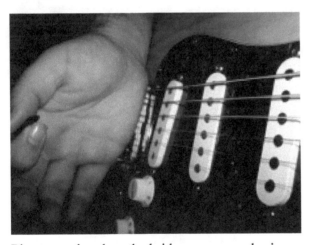

Place your hand on the bridge so your palm is muting the strings but does not dampen them.

Use your palm as an anchor to pick the strings in a downward motion to achieve the desired sound.

Palm Muting Exercises

The Following exercises will help you to practice palm muting. Practice each one slowly and make sure your hand stays in the correct position at all times. **Only palm mute where you see the section marked with the palm muting symbol, seen below.**

"P.M. ----------|."

Exercise 1

Exercise 2

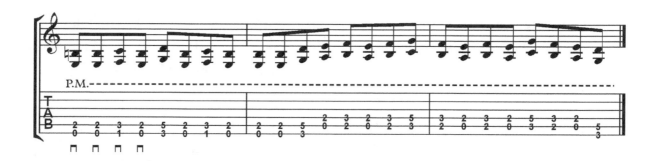

Exercise 3

Exercise 4

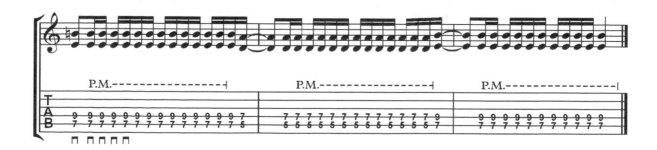

CHAPTER 12- "HAMMER ON'S", "PULL-OFF'S" AND "SLURRED" NOTES

Hammer-ons, Pull-Offs, and Slurred Notes are used to play multiple notes on the same string without picking each note.

Hammer-On's

Hammer-on's are used to move up a string from **a lower note to a higher note. A hammer-on** is created when one note is played with the 1st finger and quickly and forcefully pressing another finger down on another note on the same string without picking the note. A slurred line connecting the two notes designates a hammer-on.

Play the following exercise to get used to playing hammer-ons. The most important thing to remember when playing hammered notes is that the second note needs to be pressed hard in order to keep the volume equal between the picked note and the hammered note.

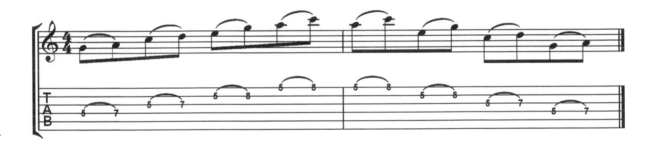

Pull-Off's

Pull-Off's are used to move down a string **from a higher note to a lower note.** A pull-off is created when one note is played and quickly and forcefully pulling the string with the fretting finger towards the ground and revealing another note played lower on the same string. **Pull-offs** are identified in music by a slurred line connecting the two notes with the letters "P.O" written below.

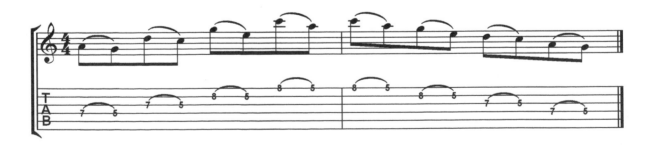

Combining Hammer-On's and Pull-Off's

The following exercise combines the use of Hammer-Ons and Pull-Offs so that you can get comfortable playing both these techniques consecutively. Hammer-Ons and Pull-Offs can be used to play a rapid series of notes and are very useful sound if played properly. Start this exercise slowly to get used to each technique and then gradually speed it up as you get comfortable.

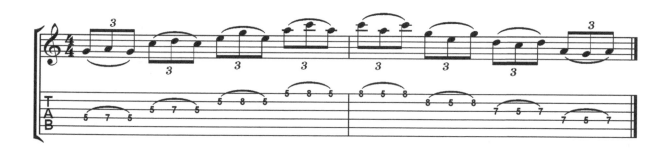

Slurred Notes

Slurred notes are played by pressing down on one note and sliding the same finger up or down the guitar neck to another note on the same string. It is important to hear the sound of your finger sliding up to the desired note, so make sure to keep the pressure on your finger all the way through the slur. The more pressure you use with your finger, the better the slur will sound

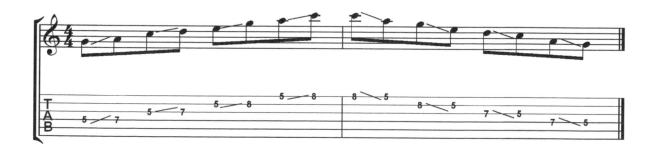

Combining Hammer-Ons, Pull-Offs, and Slurred Notes

Use these exercises to practice the combination of hammer-ons, pull-offs, and slurred notes, as they will be seen often in the same passage of a guitar solo. Make sure the volume of each note is the same as if you had picked each note.

Exercise 1

Exercise 2

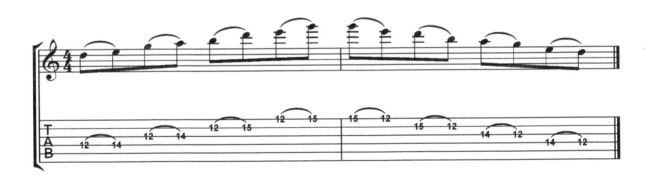

Exercise 3

CHAPTER 13 - STRING BENDING

One of the most widely used techniques in guitar playing is string bending. Similar to a **hammer-on,** string bending allows multiple notes to be played with one pick stroke. With string bending, the player literally pushes the string upward to raise the pitch to a higher pitch. This is one of the most difficult techniques to master on the guitar, because it requires a lot of strength and a lot of practice to master this technique.

With string bending, you can bend by either pushing the higher strings towards the lower strings, or pulling the lower strings towards the higher strings. Use your judgement on which direction to bend depending on the string being bent and the notes that follow.

The Four Principals of String Bending

1. Bend with your whole hand: If you are bending a note with your third finger on the third string of the guitar, place your second and first finger behind your third finger on the string and bend with all three fingers. This will give you more strength to bend the string.

2. Place your thumb on the top of the guitar neck: Use your thumb to push down on the guitar neck and to help your fingers bend the strings. Your thumb cannot be on the back of the neck with traditional playing, as your thumb will be pushing in the wrong direction to help you bend the string.

3. Keep the pressure on the string the same throughout the bend: This is important because as soon as you change the pressure on the string, the note will stop ringing. Push down on the wood of the fingerboard and try to drag your finger through the wood as you bend the string up. As you bring the bend back down, try to keep the pressure the same as well.

4. Be sure to bend the note up to the correct pitch: It is important to bend the note up to the correct pitch. Since string bends are difficult to control, this will require a lot of practice. Play the note that you are trying to reach with the bend before practicing the bend so you know what the bend should sound like.

Pay close attention to where the thumb and fingers are placed while bending!

Practice With String Bends: Half Steps

The following exercise will help you get comfortable with smaller bends before moving on to larger bends. The first type of bend we are going to learn is a half-step bend. A half-step bend is played one fret back from the desired pitch. Start slowly and make sure that the bends sound clear and on pitch before moving to the next one. Use an electronic tuner to help you match the pitch correctly.

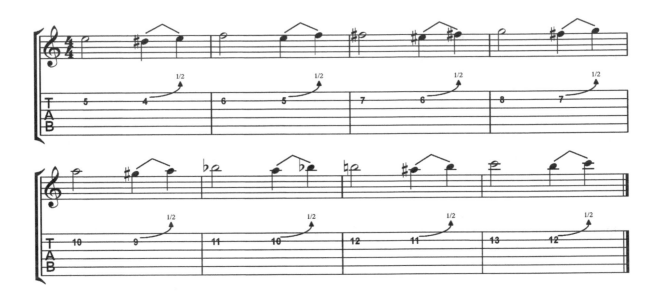

Practice With String Bends: Whole Steps

The next type of bend we are going to learn is a whole-step bend. A whole-step bend is played two frets back from the desired pitch. These bends require a lot more strength than half-step bends as they have to be bent farther to reach the desired pitch.

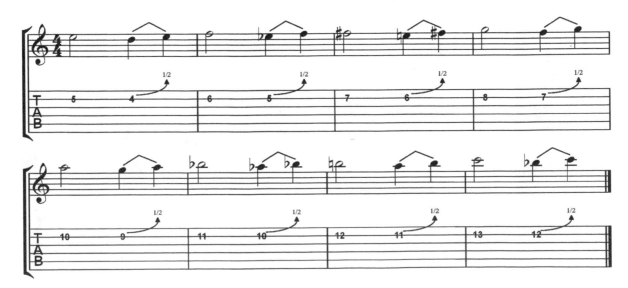

Pre-Bends

A **pre-bend** is when you bend the note up to the desired pitch before you pick the string. This gives us the illusion of bending a note down instead of up in pitch. The end result will sound similar to a **pull-off.** Pre-bends are often found in country and rock music. The bending technique is the same in the left hand, however we cannot use our ears to determine when we have achieved the desired pitch. Because of this we need to use our eyes to estimate how far to bend. Practice these bends slowly to perfect this technique. The use of an electronic tuner is encouraged to match the correct pitch.

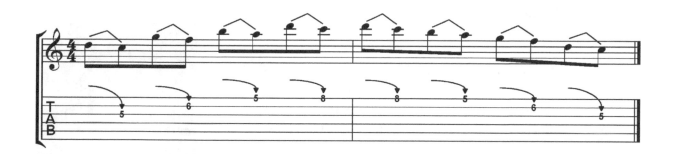

Musical Examples using String Bending

Practice the following exercises to become comfortable using string bends within the context of a guitar solo. These exercises will provide valuable ideas that can be used in guitar solos, and will get you more comfortable with string bending.

CHAPTER 14 - "FINGERSTYLE" GUITAR

Fingerstyle guitar is one of the most challenging and rewarding styles of guitar playing. This technique is found in all musical styles from jazz to rock to classical and beyond. Fingerstyle guitar differs from pick-style in several ways, most notably the absence of a flatpick (though a thumb-pick is often used) and the ability to play two or more independent lines simultaneously.

The techniques in your right and left hand require a lot of patience and practice, but the diligent student will be able to effectively integrate this technique into their repertoire and explore a whole new way of playing.

Right Hand Fingering: In order to distinguish our right hand fingering from our left hand, we use letters to represent our ringers.

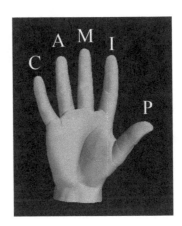

P = Thumb   **I** = Index   **M** = Middle   **A** = Ring   **C** = Pinky

Fingerstyle guitar requires a specific right hand posture and technique that is very challenging to master. Practice it slowly in order to allow your hand to get used to the position and movements.

Consider the following points when starting with this technique:

1. **Your hand should be a natural extension of your forearm:** There should be no bend between your hand and forearm to allow for maximum efficiency and muscle movement.

2. **Only touch your fingertips to the strings:** Keep your arm and wrist off the guitar and leave enough space between your hand and the guitar for your fingers to move freely.

3. **Extend your thumb in front of your hand:** Your hand position should be a relaxed fist with your thumb straight and extended in front of your hand. Your fingers should be in a soft "C" shape and never straight.

The "Touch, Rest,

Pluck" Method

The method to playing fingerstyle guitar involves a three step method to achieve the balance between good tone and projection of sound. Practice this method with each finger while paying close attention to the technique. There should be no weight in your finger, as your knuckle will push your finger through the string.

Touch: Place the fingertip and nail on the string. Your finger should be relaxed with a soft "C" shape. There should be no pressure in your fingertip and no weight resting on the string.

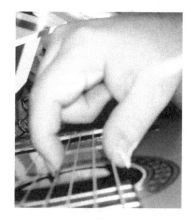

Rest: Push your finger from your knuckle and let your fingertip straighten out and rest on the string. There should be no pressure in your fingertip.

Pluck: Quickly move your finger through the string with your knuckle and back towards your palm. Angle the finger upward to avoid hitting other strings. Immediately reset your finger back to the starting position.

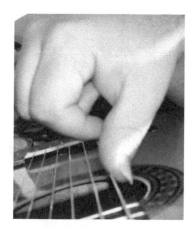

Right Hand Exercises

Practice the following exercise using the "Touch, Rest, Pluck" method. Be sure to work on each finger slowly and pay careful attention to each finger movement. You should spend about 2-3 minutes each practice session on each combination of fingerings to fully develop the technique.

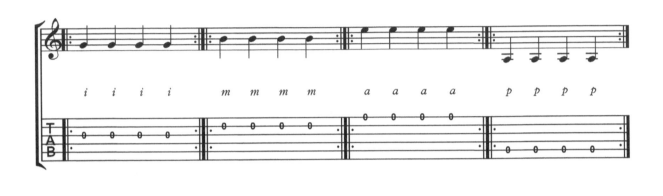

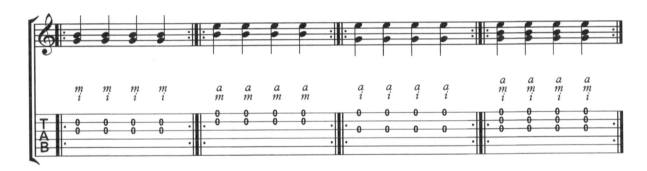

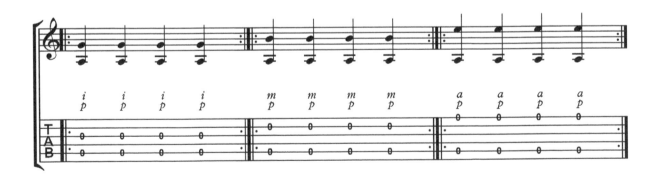

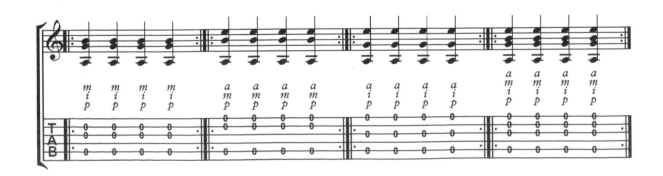

Forward Arpeggio Technique

Now that you have learned the basic fundamentals of fingerstyle technique, the next step is to work on techniques for playing forward arpeggios. An *arpeggio* is any chord played note by note sequentially rather than plucked all at once. A *forward arpeggio* is an arpeggio that moves from the bass strings to the treble strings.

To successfully play forward arpeggios, we need to separate our thumb from our three fingers. As soon as our thumb plays a bass strings, our index, middle, and ring fingers (depending on the number of notes played) will immediately and simultaneously touch the remaining strings of the arpeggio in a "spring loaded" motion. This sets up the next three notes of the arpeggio and allows for increased speed and accuracy. After the last finger plays, the thumb will immediately return to the bass note ready to start the arpeggio over again.

This alternation takes time and patience to execute correctly, and it is imperative to practice this alternation before attempting the following exercises. Don't worry about the chord progression at first and work only on the left hand. Add the chord progression in once you are comfortable with the technique.

Exercise 1

Exercise 2

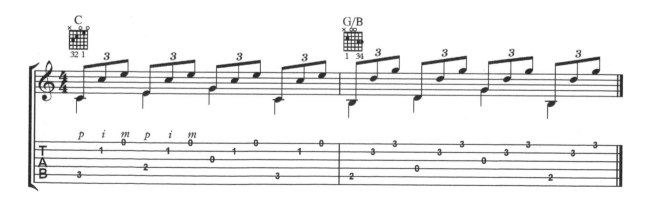

Reverse Arpeggio Technique

Unlike the forward arpeggio technique, the reverse arpeggio technique requires each finger to be played sequentially, not simultaneously. After the thumb plays the bass string, the ring finger immediately touches one of the treble strings in the same "spring loaded" fashion as with the forward arpeggio.

After the ring finger plucks through the string, the middle finger immediately follows by touching the next string. This continues with the index finger and eventually the thumb will start the arpeggio over again. This sequential motion allows the hand to stay one finger ahead of the progression and play reverse arpeggios quickly.

Just like the forward arpeggio technique, this sequential motion takes time and patience to execute correctly. Practice this alternation several times before attempting the following exercises.

Exercise 1

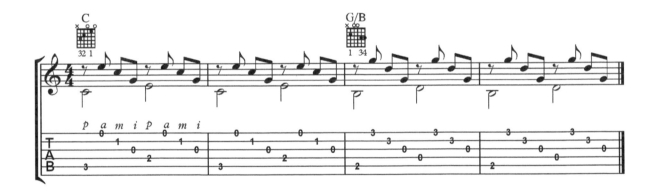

Exercise 2

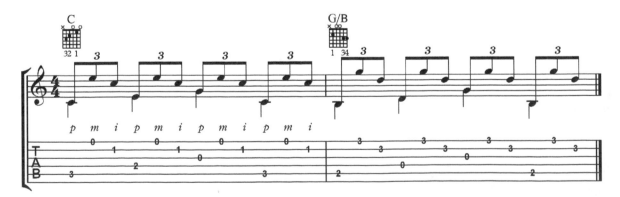

Combining Forward and Reverse Arpeggios

These exercises will help you combine what you know about forward and reverse arpeggios. Remember to use a simultaneous movement with your three fingers on the forward movement and a sequential movement for the reverse movement. Practice this slowly and carefully and remember not to move your wrist when executing these movements.

Exercise 1

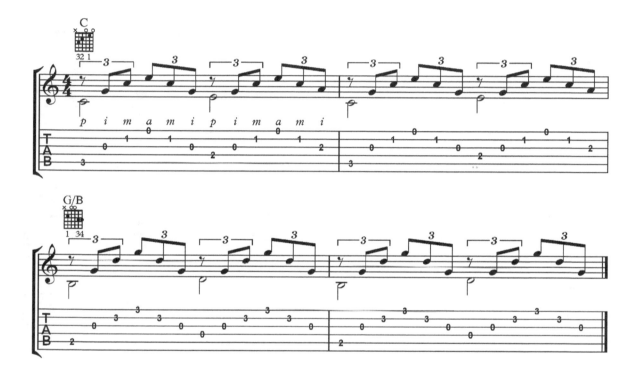

Exercise 2

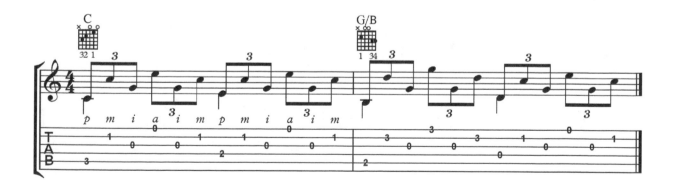

Adding The Thumb

The following exercises introduce the thumb and fingers playing together to start the arpeggio. Practice these combinations slowly to get comfortable playing two notes simultaneously. You should focus on your thumb moving independently from your three fingers.

Exercise 1

Exercise 2

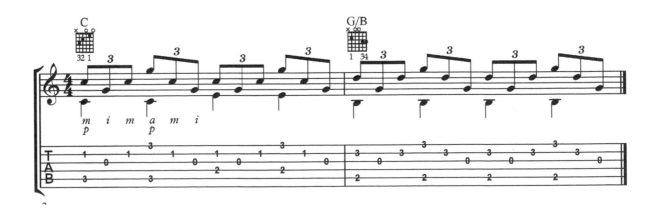

CHAPTER 15 - 7TH CHORDS AND ARPEGGIOS

All of the chords we have studied so far have been three note chords. We have learned that each chord has a root, a 3rd (which determines whether that chord is major or minor), and a 5th. By adding the 7th degree above the root to the chords that we already have, we can create chords with 4 notes in them. These chords are called 7th chords. There are four main types of 7th chords: Major 7th , Minor 7th, Dominant 7th, and Minor 7th flat 5.

Chord Type	Major 7	Dominant 7	Minor 7	Minor 7 flat 5
Formula	R, 3, 5 , 7	R, 3, 5, b7	R, b3, 5, b7	R, b3, b5, b7
Written As	Cmaj7	C7	Cm7	Cm7b5

Major 7th Chords

A major 7th chord is a major triad (Root, 3rd, 5th) with the addition of a major 7th above the root. For example, a C MAJOR 7TH chord (Cmaj7) takes the Root, 3rd, 5th, and 7th from the C major scale (C, D, E, F, G, A, B C), which gives us the notes C, E, G, and B

Cmaj7

Cmaj7

Cmaj7

Cmaj7

Cmaj7

Dominant 7th Chords

A major 7th chord is a major triad (Root, 3rd, 5th) with the addition of a lowered 7th above the root.. For example, a C DOMINANT 7th chord (C7) chord takes the Root, 3rd, 5th, and b7th, from the C major scale (C, D, E, F, G, A, B, C), which gives us the notes C, E, G, and Bb

C7

C7

C7

C7

C7

Minor 7th Chords

A minor 7th chord is a minor triad (Root, flat 3rd, 5th) with the addition of a lowered 7th above the root.. For example, a C MINOR 7th chord (Cm7) chord takes the Root, b3rd, 5th, and b7th, from the C major scale (C, D, E, F, G, A, B, C), which gives us the notes C, Eb, G, and Bb

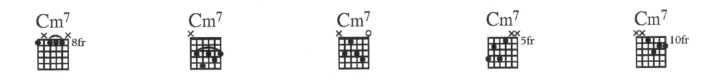

Minor 7th flat 5 Chords

A minor 7th flat 5 chord is a diminished triad (Root, flat 3rd, flat 5th) with the addition of a lowered 7th above the root. This chord is sometimes called a *Half-Diminished 7th* chord. For example, a C MINOR 7 b5 (Cm7b5) chord takes the Root, b3rd, b5th, and b7th, from the C major scale (C, D, E, F, G, A, B, C), which gives us the notes C, Eb, Gb, and Bb.

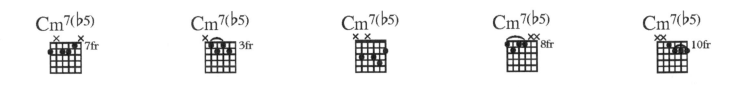

Practice the following chord progressions to better familiarize yourself with these new chord shapes.

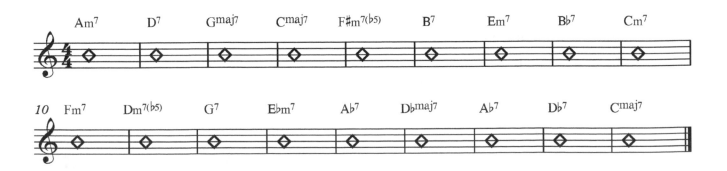

7th Chord Inversions: 6th String

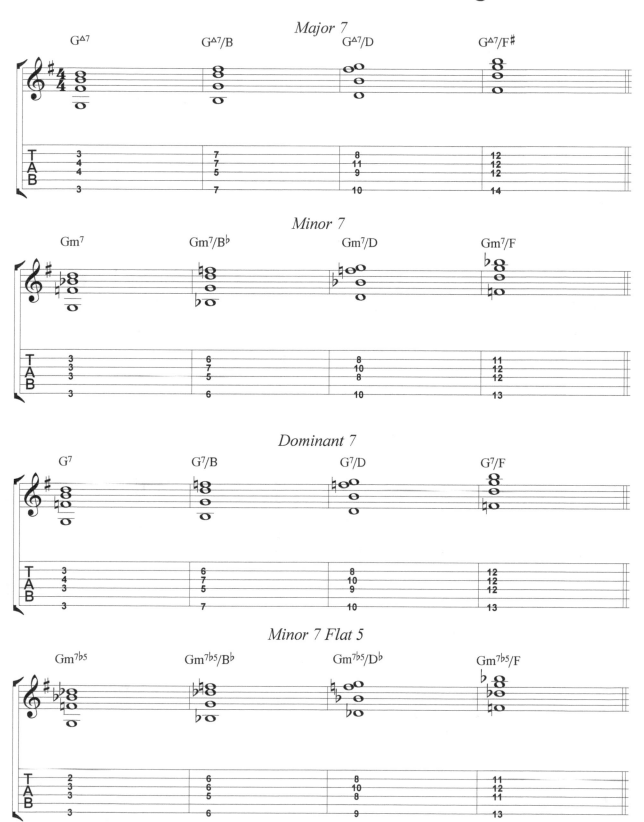

7th Chord Inversions: 5th String

Major 7

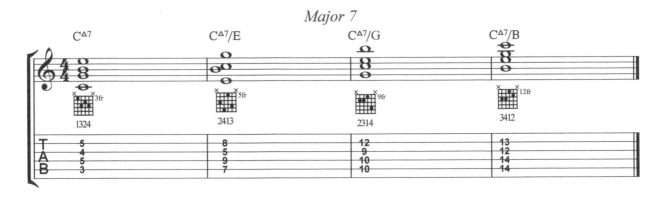

Minor 7

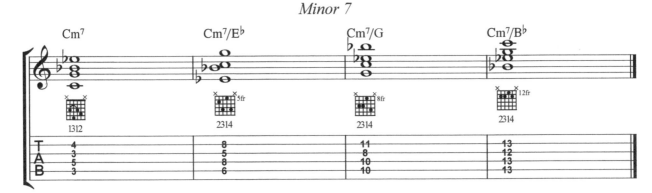

Dominant 7

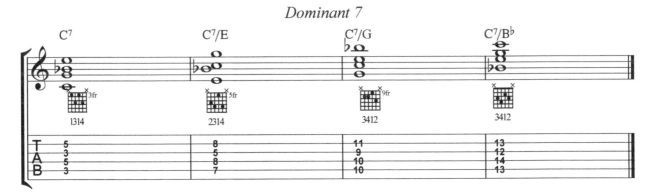

Minor 7 Flat 5

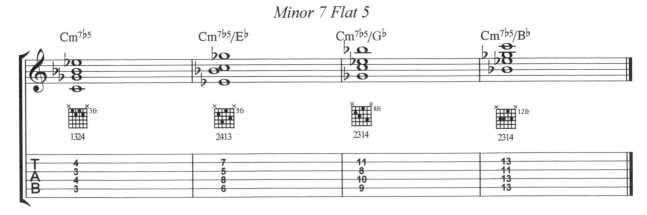

7th Chord Inversions: 4th String

Major 7

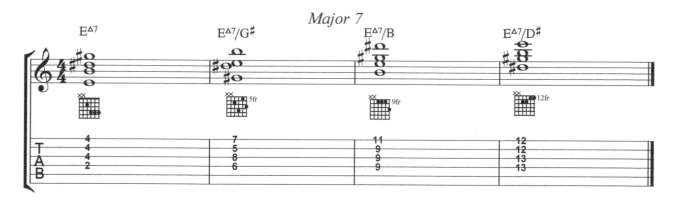

Minor 7

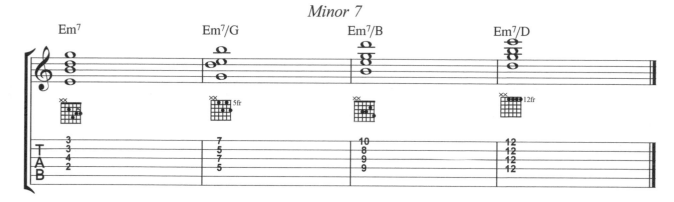

Dominant 7

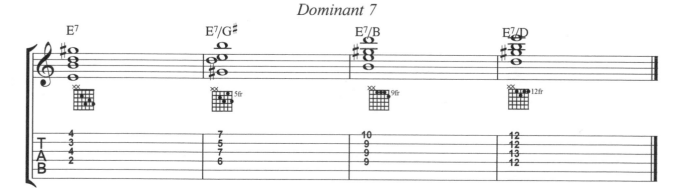

Minor 7 Flat 5

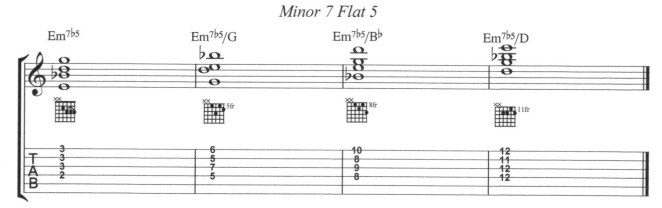

7th Chord Inversions: iim7-V7-Imaj7
6th String Root

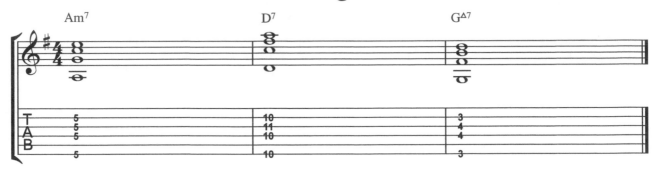

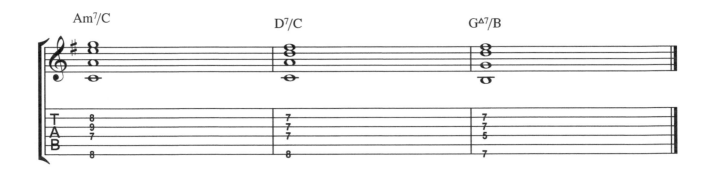

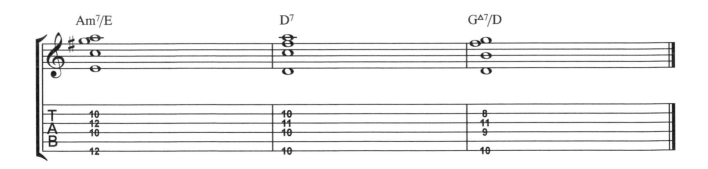

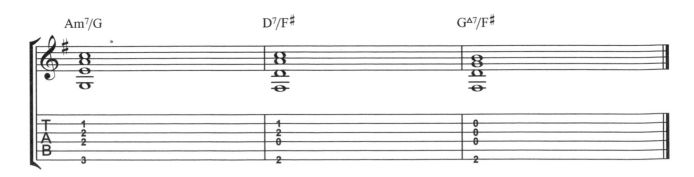

7th Chord Inversions: iim7-V7-Imaj7
5th String Root

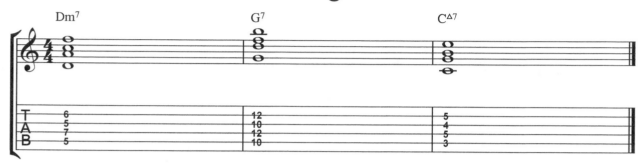

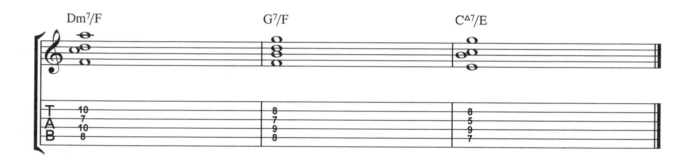

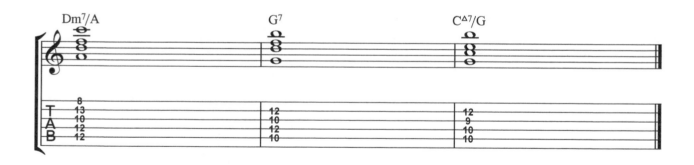

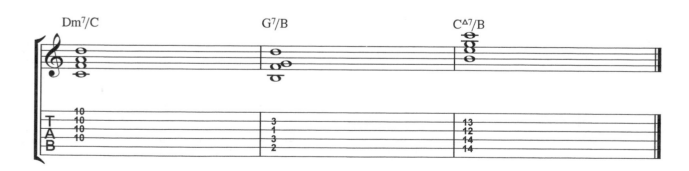

7th Chord Inversions: iim7-V7-Imaj7
4th String Root

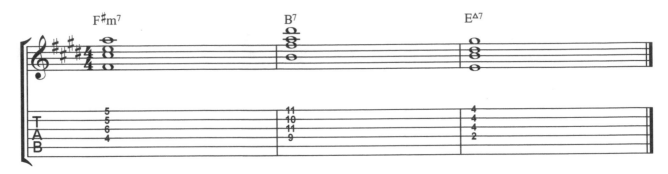

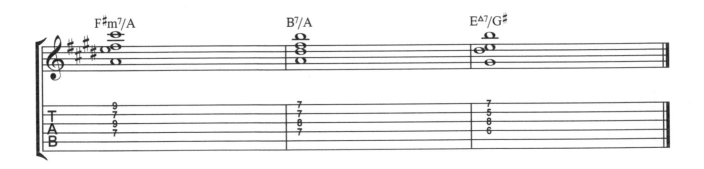

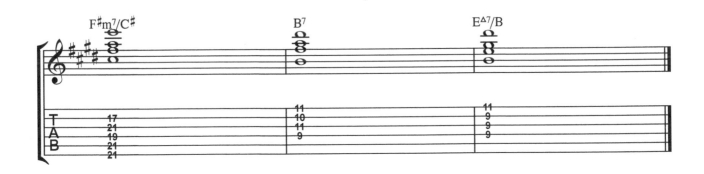

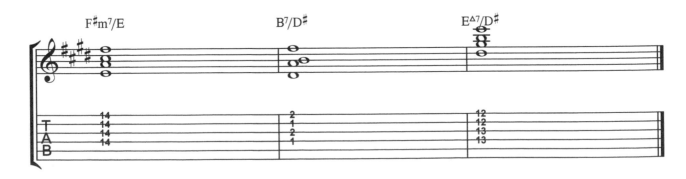

G Major 7th Arpeggio Shapes

(R,3,5,7)

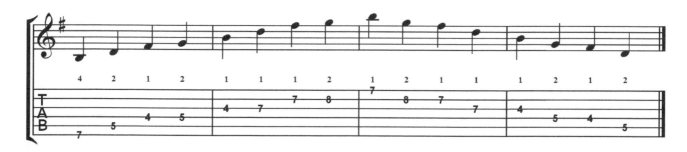

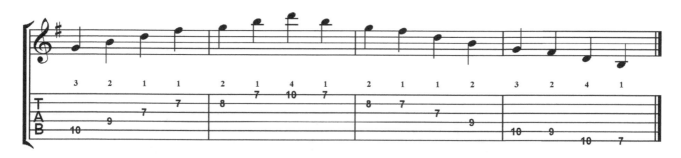

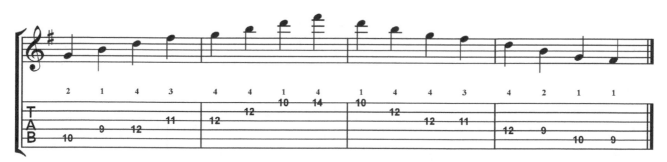

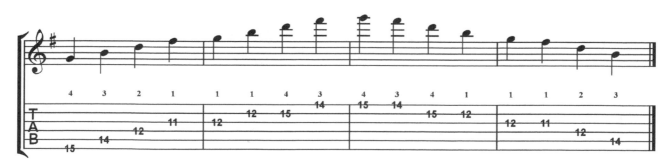

G Dominant 7th Arpeggio Shapes

(R, 3,5,♭7)

Gm7 Arpeggio Shapes

(R,b3,5,b7)

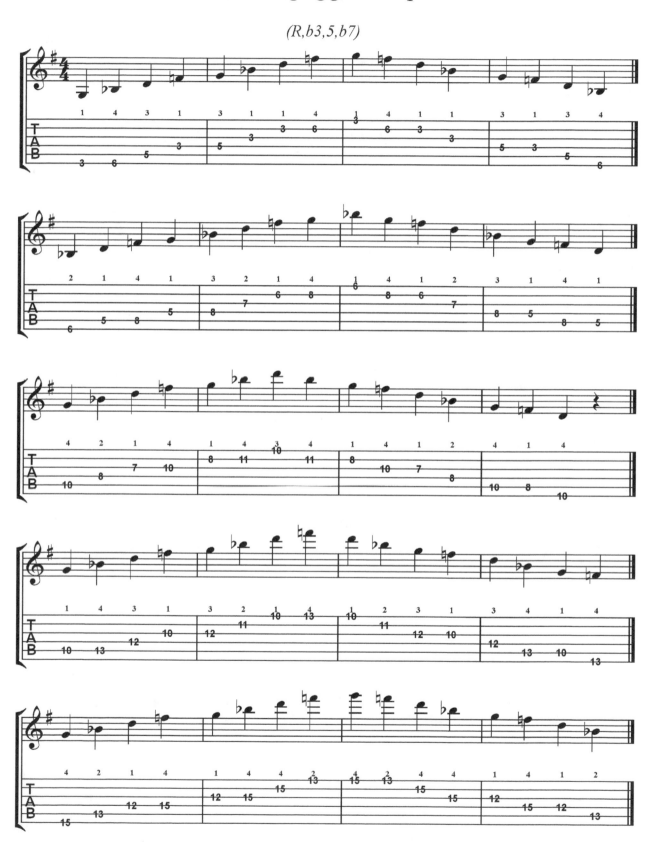

Gm7♭5 Arpeggio Shapes

(R, ♭3,♭5,♭7)

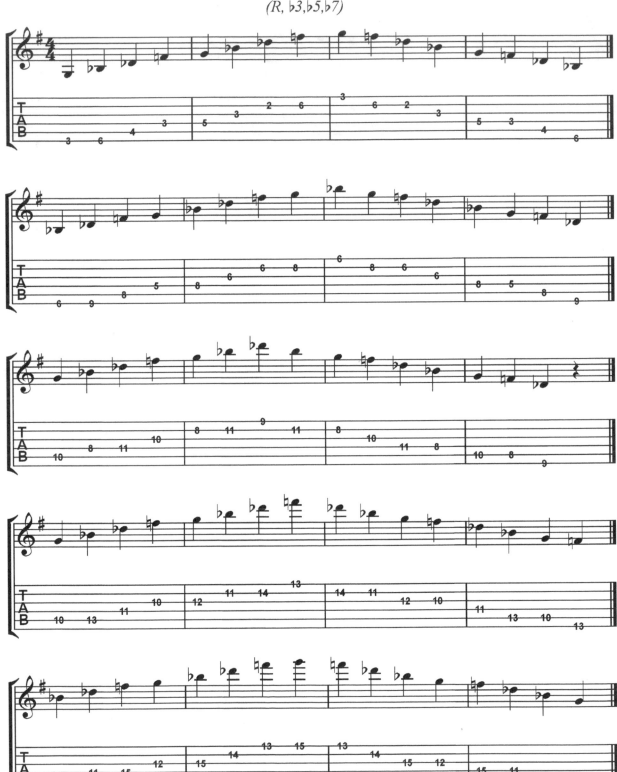

CHAPTER 16 - UPPER EXTENSION CHORDS

Some chords may contain notes other than the Root, 3rd, 5th and 7th. Rather than learning several thousand chord shapes for each upper extension, we can simply used our knowledge of the CAGED

Major	Minor	Augmented (+)	Diminished (°)
Root, 3rd, 5th	Root, $b3^{rd}$, 5th	Root, 3rd, $\#5^{th}$	Root, $b3^{rd}$, $b5^{th}$

system to find and play any chord we need.

To review, all chords are based on either a major, minor, augmented, or diminished triad. To review the different types of chords, see the chart below.

Some chords will add *Upper Extensions* to these triads. We can add the *7th, 9th (2nd), 11th (4th)*, and *13th (6th)* to any chord to create new and interesting chords. Depending on the type of chord, these extensions can be raised *(#9)* or lowered *(b9)* to further expand their harmonic capacity.

Any chord symbol, no matter how complex, is made up of three parts. For example, a Cma7 chord tells us the *Root* (C) the *Quality* (ma = major) and the extension (7)Use the following chart below to learn about different types of chords.

Major Chords

Chord Symbol	Formula
C	R, 3, 5
Csus4	R, 3, 4, 5
Cadd2, Cadd9	R, 2 (9), 3, 5
Cma6	R, 3, 5, 6
Cma7	R, 3, 5, 7
Cma9	R, 3, 5, 7, 9
Cma7#11	R, 3, 7, 9 #11
Cma13	R, 3, 5, 7, 9, 11,13

Minor Chords

Chord Symbol	Formula
Cm	R, b3, 5
Cmi7	R, b3, 5, b7
Cmi9	R, b3, 5, b7, 9
Cmi11	R, b3, 5, b7, 11
Cmi13, Cmi6	R, b3, 5, 6 (13)
Cmi(ma7)	R, b3, 5, 7

Dominant Chords

Chord Symbol	Formula
C7	R, 3, 5, b7
C9	R, 3, 5, b7, 9
C7sus	R, 3, 4, b7
C13	R, 3, 5, b7, 9, 13
C7 (b9, #9)	R, 3, 5, b7, (b9, #9)
C7 (b5 #5)	R, 3, 5, b7, (b5, #5)

When trying to create chords with these shapes, fingerings must be altered dramatically in order to correctly spell each chord. Due to the limitations of the guitar, we can only get certain notes in each chord shape. When creating these chords, we can observe a hierarchy of notes with each chord voicing. This will allow you to get all of the important notes and create very musical voicing with each chord. Practice each chord shape several times in both positions to commit it to memory.

When playing each chord listed above, observe the following rules:

• The 5th of each chord can be omitted as long as it is not altered as part of the chord

• The root can be omitted as long as it is implied by another instrument

• The 3rd and 7th define the chord quality and must be played in each voicing

• Not all extensions need to be played in each chord. A Cma7#11 only needs the R, 3rd, 7th and #11. The 9th can be omitted without losing the overall color of the chord.

• The Root of the chord does not have to be the lowest note of the voicing.

Use the examples below to find and play any chord listed above. Experiment with different fingerings to find the best possible approach to each chord. Using the above rules, you should be able to find each of the above chords in all five positions

E Major Shape with Scale Extensions

(Major Scale Position 1)

E Major Shape with Scale Extensions

(Minor Scale Position 1)

A Major Shape with Scale Extensions

(Major Scale Position 4)

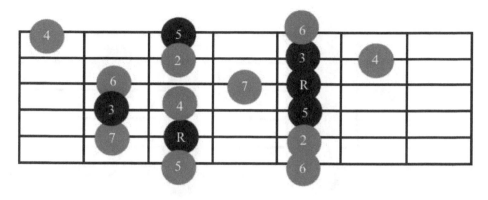

A Minor Shape with Scale Extensions

(Minor Scale Position 4)

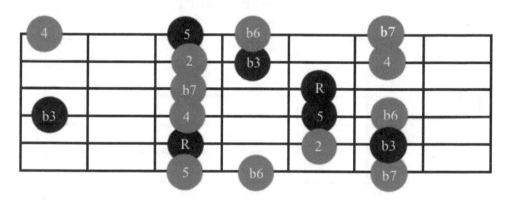

C Major Shape with Scale Extensions

(Major Scale Position 3)

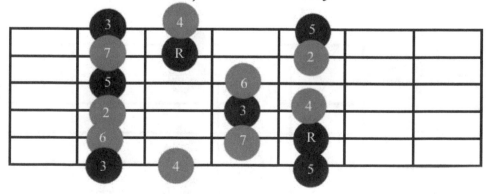

C Minor Shape with Scale Extensions

(Minor Scale Position 5)

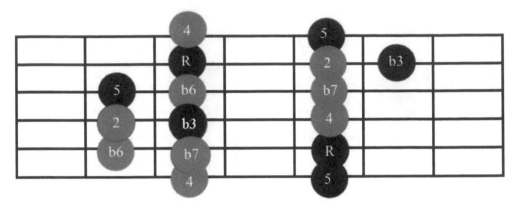

D Major Shape with Scale Extensions

(Major Scale Position 4)

G Major Shape with Scale Extensions

(Major Scale Position 5)

G Minor Shape with Scale Extensions

(Minor Scale Position 5)

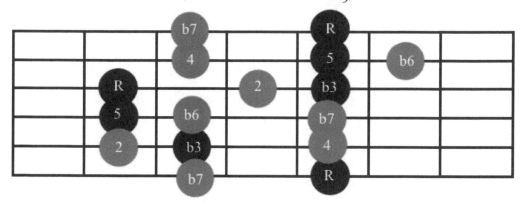

Sample Chord Shapes: Major Family 6th String

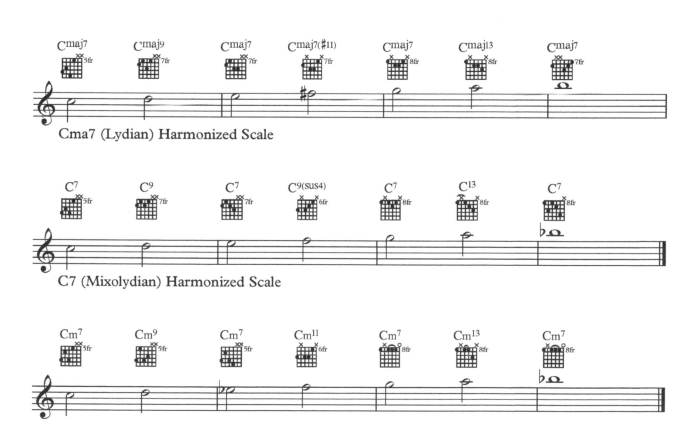

Cma7 (Lydian) Harmonized Scale

C7 (Mixolydian) Harmonized Scale

CHAPTER 17 - SWEEP PICKING

Sweep picking is one of the most advanced techniques to learn on the guitar. It will take a lot of practice and patience to get comfortable with this technique. Sweep picking is the technique of playing notes on multiple strings with the same picking attack. With sweep picking, you literally sweep the pick across the strings while articulating each note with that same pick stroke.

The main difference between sweep picking and strumming as chord is that with sweep picking, each note is fingered separately as you sweep the pick across the strings. It is very important that each note be fingered as individual notes that do not ring together as a chord.

The biggest challenge with sweep picking is to lock in the timing between the movement of the pick in the right hand and the movement of the left hand fingers. The best way to practice this technique is to work on each hand separately before connecting them together. Try fingering the exercises below with the left hand before adding the right hand and slowly sync the two together.

Downward Sweep Picking

The following exercise is designed to work on 3-string sweep picking in a downward motion. Practice very slowly until your right hand picks the note at the exact time that your left hand fingers strike the strings. After you feel comfortable with playing this exercise at a slow tempo, gradually speed up the tempo.

Upward Sweep Picking

The following exercise is designed to work on 3-string sweep picking in an upward motion. Practice very slowly until your right hand picks the note at the exact time that your left hand fingers strike the strings.

Combining Upward and Downward Sweep Picking

The following exercises are designed to combine downward and upward sweep picking. Make sure your pick and right hand are synchronized with each other.

Sweep Picking Using 4 Strings

The following exercises add the 1st string to the three from the previous exercises. Practice these slowly and carefully making sure to hear each note separately.

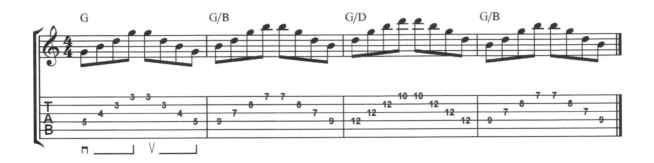

Sweep Picking Using 5 Strings

The following exercises add the 5th string to the four from the previous exercises. Practice these slowly and carefully making sure to hear each note separately.

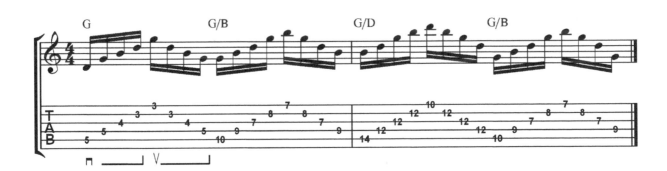

CHAPTER 18 - 9TH POSITION READING

Since the guitar has six strings, most notes on the guitar can be found in several "positions" on the fretboard. Instead of learning all of the note locations at once, we can divide the guitar into positions to help us locate the best fingering for each piece of music. We can determine the best position by studying the range (highest and lowest note) of the piece to find a suitable position

The "9th Position" refers to the notes found between the 9th and 12th frets on the guitar. This is the highest position on the neck before the positions reset at the 12th fret (with the open position notes returning one octave higher). Note the higher ledger lines and the upper range of this position. Make sure to memorize these notes before trying the exercises in this chapter.

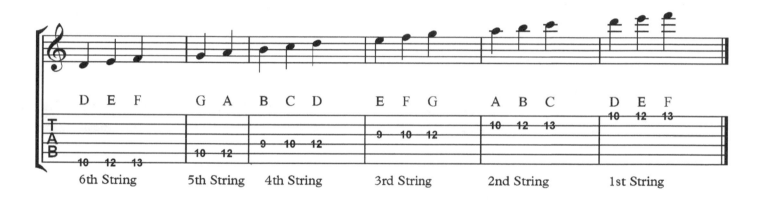

The diagram above shows the notes in the 9th position as well as their positions on the fretboard.

9th Position Reading Practice

Use the following exercise to familiarize yourself with the upper register of the guitar and reading the ledger line exercise below. With some time and practice you will be able to better recognize each note above the staff.

J.S Bach - "Violin Partita #3" in E Major